A Guide to United Kingdom and European Union
Competition Policy

Also by Nick Gardner

DECADE OF DISCONTENT

A Guide to
United Kingdom and
European Union
Competition Policy

Nick Gardner

Third Edition

First edition (*A Guide to United Kingdom and European Community
Competition Policy*) 1990
Second edition 1996
Third edition 2000

Published by
MACMILLAN PRESS LTD
Houndmills, Basingstoke, Hampshire RG21 6XS
and London
Companies and representatives
throughout the world

ISBN 0–333–76391–2

A catalogue record for this book is available
from the British Library.

This book is printed on paper suitable for recycling and
made from fully managed and sustained forest sources.

10   9   8   7   6   5   4   3   2   1
09 08 07 06 05 04 03 02 01 00

Printed and bound in Great Britain by
Antony Rowe Ltd, Chippenham, Wiltshire

To my family

Contents

Preface

With the passing of the Competition Act 1998, compliance with competition law has ceased to be a matter for specialists. Every major company is expected to train and inform all those employees whose activities may be touched by competition law. Smaller companies that may be damaged by the anticompetitive behaviour of their larger rivals will also wish their senior executives to be made aware of the remedies that are available. Evasion of competition law has ceased to be a low-risk, penalty-free commercial strategy. Powers of entry and search have reduced the prospects of concealment. Infringements – even if contrary to explicit company instructions – now attract heavy financial penalties, and obstruction is a criminal offence.

These legislative changes will not, for the most part, alter the attitudes of the regulatory authorities toward particular business practices. Past decisions of the British authorities, although not intended to set precedents, continue to throw some light upon their future attitudes, but the precedents set by decisions of the European authorities now have an overruling impact upon domestic practice. There have been signs, however, of a more relaxed attitude toward commercial relations between manufacturers and distributors and between licensors and licensees. Recent decisions in those areas must therefore be given more weight than older precedents.

This book is intended as a practical guide to the decisions of the regulatory authorities. It is written for business executives, not for their legal or economic advisers. It is concerned with legal procedures and economic theories only to the extent that they affect the treatment of specific business practices. Its purpose is to provide the reader with a comprehensive and rapidly accessible guide to the business conduct which the authorities consider acceptable. It takes particular categories of commercial practice in turn, and examines their treatment under the law – the reverse of the direction adopted by legal texts. No previous knowledge of law or economics is required: introductory summaries provide all the background information that is needed, and every technical term is explained. The coverage of business conduct is comprehensive, in that every regulated business practice is included. It is not, however, exhaustive. It covers a range of the circumstances under which each practice has been investigated but it was not practicable to deal in detail with every possible combination of relevant circumstances. Where further relevant information is available, a reference or a footnote indicates where it can be found, and there is guided access to over 300 cases. Nearly all the additional information that may be required can be found – or can be ordered – on the Internet.

The reader is invited to explore the contents of this book either consecutively or selectively. A businessman whose concern is with a particular commercial transaction may wish to go straight to the chapter in Part II which surveys the treatment of that type of transaction, and then, if necessary, to consult the relevant case reports among those referred to.[1] If he then feels the need to understand more about the reasons for the attitudes of the authorities, or about the way in which they conduct their business, he may wish to return to some of the sections of Part I for an outline of the intellectual, legislative or administrative framework within which they operate. The reader who is more concerned to get a general understanding of how the system works may prefer to start his reading here, and where necessary to skip through those sections of Parts I and II which treat particular topics in more detail than he requires. The general reader may then wish to turn to the survey in Part III of the past achievements and the possible future development of competition policy. The cross-referencing is designed to enable a reader to start anywhere he wishes, and to direct him to whatever additional explanations he may need in order to understand what he reads. Technical terms are defined in notes when they first occur, and also in an appendix, for the benefit of readers who encounter them later.

---

1 It is intended that cases referred to in the main text, rather than in footnotes, be consulted whenever the reader is uncertain about the authorities' attitude to a particular business practice.

Part I

The Framework of Competition Policy

1
Ideas and Their Implementation

A Introduction

The legislative framework of competition policy provides no more than a broad indication of the intentions of the policymakers who devised it. It delegates to the authorities which it appoints, a wide range of discretion in their performance of the task of giving practical effect to those intentions. That discretion is not exercised in a vacuum, however: those responsible are influenced by the intellectual and political climate and by the social and constitutional environment within which they operate. This chapter is concerned with the nature of those influences.

The principal intellectual influence upon legislators, as well as upon those appointed to implement their policies, has of course been economic theory. It would be difficult indeed to find another branch of public policy so thoroughly dominated by a set of abstract theoretical propositions. The original basis for competition policy was a set of propositions concerning competition which were first put forward by nineteenth-century economists; and those propositions continue to constitute what might be termed the 'mainstream view' of its rationale. They are founded, however, on a highly simplified model of the economy, and of the workings of firms within it; and even within that model, they are subject to important qualifications which are often overlooked. In recent years, moreover, the use of that model as the rationale for competition policy has come under attack, and fresh theoretical developments have begun to have their influence. Section B, below, is a non-technical résumé of the relevant propositions of mainstream competition theory and of its assumptions and limitations.

Competition policy need not, however, be exclusively concerned with the promotion of competition. Other objectives are also sought in the

3

British system, and in most of the other regulatory systems. The choice of objectives can have a profound influence upon the practical working of a system, as can the choices which are made among the various possible modes of implementation. Those choices are discussed in section C of this chapter.

B   The economic rationale

Perfect competition

The merit of starting with the economists' concept of *perfect competition* is that it describes a situation which can readily be analysed to give some definite and straightforward answers. The concept refers, however, to a special set of circumstances which may in two senses be regarded as idealistic. In the first place, the circumstances themselves are so special that they are not often encountered in the real world. Secondly, the economic consequences of those circumstances turn out to be optimal in a precisely definable sense. Thus the imaginary world of perfect competition turns out also to be the best of all possible worlds.

The hypothetical world with which the concept of perfect competition is concerned is one in which the market for each category of product has the following characteristics.

(a)   *All market shares are small.* No supplier enjoys a share of the market which is large enough to enable him to influence the price of that category of product.
(b)   *No collusion.* Each supplier acts independently.
(c)   *No barriers to entry.* There is nothing to prevent any new supplier from entering the market for any category of product.
(d)   *Homogeneity of product.* All suppliers of each category of product are known by all buyers to supply identical products.

Suppliers are assumed to maximise their profits, and buyers are assumed to seek value for money. After a settling-down period, a market price emerges for each category of product. A supplier who attempts to sell a product at above that price will find no buyers, and a customer who attempts to buy a product at below that price will find no sellers.

Those characteristics define the conditions for perfect competition among suppliers of products. They may similarly be defined in relation to suppliers of labour. And for pure competition to apply to the market as a whole, conditions analogous to (a) and (b) must also be satisfied by buyers: there must be no dominant buyers, and buyers must not collude.

Economics textbooks analyse the consequences of perfect competition for buyers and for sellers.[1] The term *optimal resource allocation* is used to describe the theoretical outcome for the community as a whole. In non-technical language, this can be taken to mean the efficient allocation of resources as between different categories of product. Perfect competition ensures that the community's resources are used efficiently in the sense of making people feel well-off. If resources are allocated optimally, then people would not, for example, feel better off if they were able to afford more meat and less fish, nor vice versa.[2]

A word of caution about terminology is needed at this point. The temptation to assert that perfect competition maximises economic efficiency must be resisted because the theory outlined above makes purely formal assumptions about *productive efficiency*.[3] Nor is it strictly correct to say that perfect competition maximises economic welfare. The concept of *economic welfare*[4] encompasses the way in which wealth is distributed as between different members of the community, and it cannot be claimed that perfect competition necessarily leads to an ideal distribution of wealth. The propositions which emerge from the concept of perfect competition are to do with the way in which resources are allocated between products, and not with how the product is manufactured, or to whom it is distributed.

Externalities

One further qualification is needed. The outcome will not necessarily be efficient if any supplier can impose costs on others. In economics jargon, these are termed *externalities*.[5] The conventional example is a supplier who pollutes the environment. The allocation of resources need not then be efficient because of the possibility that some people would feel better off with fewer goods in exchange for a cleaner atmosphere. Other examples include traffic congestion and mining subsidence. The theoretically ideal solution is for the polluter to compensate those affected; and if this is practicable, it takes the matter outside the scope of competition policy. Considerations of practicability may, however, occasionally require competition policy to take externalities

---

[1] For example, Baumol 1961.
[2] More precisely, the term means that there can be no reallocation of resources which would make anyone better off without making someone worse off.
[3] The efficiency with which resources are combined to produce a specific product.
[4] Readers who wish to pursue the complications introduced by the concept of economic welfare should consult Winch 1971 or Little 1957.
[5] Consequences for welfare which are not reflected in costs and prices.

into account and to attempt to remedy the resulting distortion of consumer choice.

Perfect monopoly and oligopoly

The importance of the concept of perfect competition to the philosophy of competition policy is that it serves as a datum, or baseline, from which the departures which occur in the real world can be measured. It defines one of the polar extremes of possible real-world situations. The other polar extreme is *perfect monopoly* – that is to say, a product market in which the product has only one supplier and into which no other supplier can enter. Like perfect competition, this is a situation which can readily be analysed to produce unequivocal results. The diagrammatic analysis which appears in the standard economic textbooks demonstrates that under these circumstances the profit-maximising supplier would provide smaller quantities of the product, and at a higher price, than would be the case under perfect competition. The mechanism which leads to that unsurprising conclusion is of more interest than the conclusion itself. It rests on the fact that the monopolist always has the freedom to choose between supplying a greater quantity at a lower price and supplying a smaller quantity at a higher price.[6]

The existence of such choices is said to confer *market power* upon the supplier in question. The possession of market power in that sense is not, however, confined to perfect monopolies. There are many markets in the real world in which there are several suppliers, each of which is large enough to enjoy a degree of market power in the sense of having some degree of choice concerning pricing policy. A great deal of theoretical work has been done on the subject but straight-forward answers concerning the behaviour of a profit-maximising supplier in such an *oligopolistic* market are hard to find. The reason is that analysis of such markets is complicated by the need to postulate how each supplier reacts to the likely behaviour of his competitors, and by the need for a precise understanding of each supplier's cost structure.

Since competition policy has to deal mainly with markets which operate under neither pure competition nor pure monopoly, these difficulties create a dilemma. Is it satisfactory to simplify the analysis by treating the real world as a mixture of many markets ruled by

---

[6] Those choices are represented in the textbooks as a *downward-sloping demand curve* and the diagrammatic analysis shows the profit-maximising price to be jointly determined by that curve and the supplier's cost curve.

something approximating to perfect competition, together with a few others which approximate to pure monopoly? Or is it necessary to abandon that unrealistic simplification and tackle the formidable problems of analysing oligopoly as it occurs in practice? In the postwar debate over this dilemma, the simplified approach was successfully defended by Milton Friedman on the grounds that the value of any piece of analysis depends, not upon the realism of its underlying assumptions, but upon its ability to yield useful results (Friedman 1966). It was generally concluded that perfect competition and pure monopoly theory, applied with qualifications dictated by common sense, would yield a satisfactory theoretical basis for competition policy. That – at least, until recently – is how the matter was left.

The second-best

Apart from the problems of living with the artificial assumptions underlying conventional competition theory, there is one problem which is inherent in that theory. The theory's most telling conclusion is that if universal perfect competition is taken as the starting-point, any departure from it will lead to a loss of economic efficiency. But, if the starting-point is one in which some markets are not perfectly competitive, it cannot be concluded that efficiency would be increased by restoring any one of them to perfect competition. This is not a finicky academic point, moreover; it is a matter of some practical importance. It is not hard to see that it might be better from the consumer's standpoint to have a monopoly supplier of coal, faced with a monopoly supplier of electricity as his main customer, rather than an alternative in which the coal supplier would be free to exploit his monopoly power in dealings with a fragmented electricity supply industry.[7]

The *theory of the second-best*, as this is called, may seem seriously to undermine the intellectual foundations of competition policy, but in practice its implications are often less formidable. There is a clear need to take account of linkages between markets such as exist between the markets for coal and electricity – and this can often be successfully tackled by a mixture of analysis and common sense. Also, there are many instances in which such linkages are so weak that the direct benefits of an increase in competition in one market would clearly outweigh any adverse secondary effect. Cases are bound to arise, nonetheless, in which there is no analytical solution to the problem of the second-best.

---

[7] In a market dominated by a major supplier, a merger between two of his rivals might similarly provide a *second-best solution* and examples of this are discussed in Chapter 5.

Policy prescriptions

The economic rationale of competition policy which is set out in the above résumé has been concerned with what might be termed *mainstream competition theory*. That mainstream theory does not, however, provide the only possible rationale for competition policy. A number of alternative theories of competition have been advanced over the years, some of which are now beginning to influence the conduct of competition policy. Since the practical relevance of those other strands of competition theory is determined by the extent to which they yield different policy-prescriptions, the time has come to review the prescriptive implications of the mainstream theory.

Since departure from any of the four conditions for perfect competition listed on page 4 leads in theory to a loss of efficiency, the possible prescriptive implications of the theory might be categorised as follows.

(a)   *Action to restrict market shares*. This might include controls on mergers, and the breaking-up of large firms.

(b)   *Prohibition of collusion*. This could include the prohibition of any of a wide range of practices which limit competition among existing firms.

(c)   *Removal of entry barriers*. Action could range from the prohibition of suppliers' practices which discourage entry, to positive action to promote entry.

(d)   *Measures to improve information*. The measures might seek to prevent suppliers from misleading their customers, and they might also seek positively to inform customers.

In case of uncertainty concerning the effectiveness of the above, a fifth category would be:

(e)   *Price control*. This would seek to compel a supplier to set prices at the levels which would rule under perfect competition.

Such policy actions may, however, result in a loss of *productive efficiency*,[8] tending to offset the resulting gains in *allocative efficiency*,[9] and the policies concerned with the promotion of economic welfare must involve the balancing of those gains and losses.

---

[8] The efficiency with which resources are combined to produce a specific product.
[9] The efficiency with which resources are allocated as between different products.

Vertical and horizontal transactions

Competition theory draws an important distinction between *horizontal*[10] and *vertical*[11] transactions. Whereas most horizontal mergers and agreements have a direct and unequivocal effect upon market power, the effects of vertical transactions are often indirect and conditional upon the extent of existing market power. Restrictions such as exclusive distribution can, for example, be used by a manufacturer to extend his market power, but they are unlikely to be effective unless he already possesses substantial market power. Such restrictions have often been condemned in the belief that they offered no gains in productive efficiency to offset their possible detrimental effects upon allocative efficiency. Studies[12] done in the 1980s and 1990s which recognise that manufacturing and retailing are both part of the production process, have however, used game theory to analyse the advantages[13] obtainable from such restrictions. While the prohibition of some vertical restraints, such as retail price maintenance, is likely to continue, these findings have led to a more permissive attitude toward the generality of vertical agreements.

The competitive process

Critics have argued that the entire rationale of mainstream competition theory is flawed by virtue of its methodology. That methodology, which is termed *comparative statics*, envisages a system which settles down to a stable equilibrium. The properties of that equilibrium are then analysed as though it were a static situation. In reality, of course, the postulated settling-down process may never end. New techniques and new products may emerge in a continuing stream; new firms may come into existence to turn the resulting opportunities into reality, and other firms may fail. Above all, there are uncertainties; and entrepreneurs are rewarded – if successful – for taking risks. None of those vital characteristics of the competitive process can be embodied in a comparative statics analysis. Consequently, it is argued, that form of analysis is inappropriate to the problem.

The principal proponents of that line of argument are the *Austrian School* of economists, and their case is more extensively summarised in Littlechild (1986) and Reekie (1979).

---

[10] Transactions between competitors.
[11] For instance, transactions between manufacturers and retailers or between licensees and licensors, such as are described in Chapter 7.
[12] Summarised in Dobson and Waterson 1996 and in the European Commission's *Green Paper on Vertical Restraints*.
[13] For example, avoidance of under-promotion resulting from *free-rider* behaviour by retailers.

A possible prescription for competition policy which follows from a full acceptance of the above argument is total inaction on the grounds that the analysis necessary for successful intervention is so complex, and the necessary information so hard to come by, that intervention is as likely to do harm as to do good. An alternative prescription is temporary inaction pending further analytical and empirical developments. The more pragmatic members of the Austrian School are prepared to countenance active competition policy, but counsel a cautious approach which recognises the complexity of the real world and the consequent dangers of error; and which therefore intervenes only in the most clear-cut of cases.

Contestability

Competition theory was augmented in the 1970s by analytical developments in which the concept of perfect competition was replaced as a benchmark by the concept of *perfect contestability*. This has provided a new way of looking at competition.

A *perfectly contestable market*[14] was defined as one into which entry is absolutely free and exit is absolutely costless. If the initial outlays required for entry to a market were recoverable without loss, then any risk which might otherwise attach to entry could be eliminated. A new supplier who could see a profitable opportunity of entering a market in which prices had previously been raised by the exercise of market power would be aware that those prices would be likely to fall again as a result of his entry. But, given the opportunity of costless exit, that would not deter him from entering. There would be nothing to lose, provided that he remained in the market for only so long as it continued to be profitable to do so. Faced by such a threat, a monopoly supplier in a perfectly contestable market would thus be deterred from setting his prices at above the level which would rule under perfect competition by the knowledge that to do so would be to encourage entry. If successful entry actually occurred, he would eventually be forced to reduce his prices to the level which would rule under perfect competition in order to survive.

Thus if a market is found to be perfectly contestable – or nearly so – the authorities need do nothing, and might do harm by intervening. If it is not fully contestable, then the preferred action is to attempt to remove the obstacles to contestability. If contestability cannot be

---

[14] The theory and its policy implications are examined in Baumol 1982 and in Baumol, Panzar and Willig 1982.

guaranteed, however, there remains a case for applying the prescription of conventional competition theory. Any disadvantages of intervention – including, particularly, any discouragement offered to potential entrants – should, however, be carefully weighed against its likely benefits.

The practical implications of the theory of contestability have turned out to be very limited.[15] It was thought at first that perfect contestability might be closely approached in the real world. Promising examples were expected to be found in the deregulated United States airline industry – but further investigations[16] have called this into question. It is clear that the existence of 'sunk costs' – such as the irrecoverable costs of promoting customer awareness of a new product – is a serious obstacle.

Limitations of the rationale

Competition theory provides the intellectual foundation for competition policy but it does not provide all that is needed to build a serviceable structure upon that foundation. It does not lead to unequivocal prescriptions except where competition is the only question at issue – and even then the questions of externalities and of 'the second-best' may introduce qualifications. Where the issue of gains in productive efficiency also arises, other branches of economic theory must be called in aid. The difficulties which then arise stem not so much from the limitations of the available theory, as from the fact that quantification is then needed in order to draw up a balance between losses of allocative efficiency and gains of productive efficiency. The analytical framework for such calculations is available, but the information requirements for a successful analysis tend to be demanding, and commercial accounting systems are seldom capable of providing the necessary inputs.

In practical terms, therefore, the economic rationale for competition policy is incomplete and, at best, its implementation depends partly upon judgement rather than entirely upon analysis. A very substantial programme of empirical work[17] would be needed to repair those deficiencies.

C   Objectives and their implementation

The economic rationale which has been outlined above provides the intellectual justification for the proposition that competition policy can be used to increase economic efficiency. It does not, however, lead to

---

[15] As noted by Schwartz 1986.
[16] For instance, Morrison and Winston 1987.
[17] Such as that proposed by Baumol, Panzar and Willig 1982, p. 467.

any unique prescription for its implementation. Different administrations have developed widely differing systems of implementation, despite their common rationale. The differences arise from the choices which have been made concerning the range of objectives to be served, and concerning the means which may be chosen to achieve them.

Objectives

Competition theory indicates that individual businessmen may find it in their shareholders' interests to do things which are harmful to the community as a whole. If this were the only issue, and if intervention on behalf of the community could be confined to prohibiting those anti-competitive actions, then the choice of policy objectives would be straightforward. The complicating factor is the possibility that some anti-competitive behaviour may not be unequivocally harmful.

It is noted above that the type of economic efficiency which, in competition theory, is diminished by a departure from pure competition is *allocative efficiency*; and that there may also be beneficial effects upon *productive efficiency*. There may sometimes be a case for adopting the presumption that effects on allocative efficiency will predominate unless the contrary can be demonstrated. Such a presumption can make it difficult, if not impossible, to defend any action which reduces competition. In the context of a heavily cartelised industry structure – such as was perceived to exist in the United States in the late nineteenth century – it might even seem sensible to concentrate upon improving allocative efficiency by attacking anti-competitive structures and practices, regardless of any possible loss of productive efficiency. There are still some remnants of that approach in present-day United States anti-trust policy.[18] To the extent that such a policy is successful, however, the case for persisting with it is weakened. A reaction against the excesses which can arise under such a policy may lend plausibility to the opposite extreme of not intervening against a reduction of competition unless action can be taken without any loss of productive efficiency.

If the promotion of competition is not to be the sole objective of competition policy, then other objectives must be formulated. A more ambitious objective would be to increase economic welfare – a concept which encompasses productive as well as allocative efficiency, but which also includes the controversial subject of the distribution of

---

[18] As noted in section D below.

wealth. The lack of a precise criterion for wealth distribution is an obstacle to such an extension, but its place might be taken by a consensus in favour, for example, of greater equality, the alleviation of unemployment, or the promotion of small firms.

The policy objectives need not be confined to economic goals; competition policy may be used also to promote wider social and political objectives. The British concept of *the public interest*[19] embraces a number of specified considerations, and leaves it to the regulatory authority to take into account any further considerations as it thinks fit. There was also provision in the Treaty of Rome[20] for consideration to be given to wider social consequences.

Rules, discretion and delegation

The chosen objectives may be sought either by the general enforcement of predetermined rules of conduct, or by a case-by-case exercise of discretion. The constitutional traditions of western civilisation favour rules-based enforcement because of its advantages in terms of transparency and accountability. The formulation of the legendary twelve tables of Roman law is said to have been proposed by the tribune Terentillus so that the ruling consuls would be 'bound to use against the people only the authority granted to them by popular consent, instead of giving the force of law, as they do at present, to their own arbitrary passions' (Livy). From the early days of the Roman Republic, lip-service at least has been given to the precept that government may not interfere with the affairs of the citizen except on the basis of a code of law, which is accessible to all. Departures from that precept have, however, been increasingly necessary because of the increasing complexity of life and the consequent inability of legislatures to anticipate all of the circumstances under which their legislation is to apply. There nevertheless remains a constitutional presumption against the unnecessary use of discretionary methods of enforcement.

There are some business practices which can be regulated without difficulty by the enforcement of simple rules. Generally speaking, they consist of those easily defined practices, which are considered to be harmful under all circumstances. But it is difficult to frame precise rules to deal with practices which are harmful only under particular circumstances, or only when carried to excess. Where matters of such complexity arise, some exercise of discretion is virtually inevitable. The

---

[19] See Annex 2.1 to Chapter 2.
[20] Arts 2 and 3 and Rehearsal 13 to Regulation 4064/89.

choices which then remain are those concerning what limits are to be placed upon the exercise of that discretion, who is to exercise it, and what procedures they are to adopt.

In a system in which there is no statutory delegation of powers of discretion to ministers or to specialised agencies, it falls to the courts of law to exercise discretion on matters of substance as well as on matters of legal interpretation. Statutory delegation may be preferable where technical issues are involved which are considered to be beyond the competence of the courts. The delegation of statutory powers to agencies, rather than to ministers, can have the advantage of taking the exercise of discretion outside the scope of parliamentary debate, and thus of limiting the danger that decisions might be influenced by short-term political considerations. In the absence of parliamentary control, a measure of protection against the arbitrary, unfair or irrational exercise of discretionary powers may be provided by a provision for appeal to the courts, but it is in the nature of the reasons for the appointment of a special agency that the courts would not normally overrule the agency on matters of professional judgement.

Where discretion is exercised by a statutory agency, that agency may be empowered within statutory limits to issue its own rules or guidelines, and its decisions may in time have the practical effect – if not the legal effect – of setting precedents. The true effect of the delegation of discretionary powers may thus be the eventual emergence of a well-founded and generally understood code of acceptable behaviour concerning a wide range of business practices.

Form and effect

Whether rules-based or discretionary, a regulatory system requires clear definitions of the practices which fall within its scope. A practice may be defined for that purpose either in terms of its form, or in terms of its effect. An example of the application of a form-based or *per se* definition would be the prohibition of exclusive dealing (the practice of making it a condition of supply that a retailer does not deal with other suppliers). A form-based definition of that sort has the merit of letting all concerned know exactly where they stand. It also simplifies regulation by excluding all considerations other than the evidence concerning the existence of the practice. However, it invites the use of devices which meet the letter of the law but evade its intent. A loyalty rebate could, in the example, be used to obtain the equivalent of exclusive dealing without breaching the form-based prohibition of that practice. An attempt to amend the form-based rules to prevent companies from evading the intent of the policy may result in an unending contest between the drafters of legislation and the company lawyers.

A prohibition of practices which have the effect of exclusive dealing could not be evaded in that way, and that alternative has the merit of directly attacking the real problem. On the other hand, the use of an effects-based prohibition introduces an element of judgement into the implementation of policy, which may reduce its certainty. The circumstances under which a quantity discount would be deemed to have the prohibited effect might, in the example, be unclear. In the longer term, however, many such uncertainties might be expected to be resolved by the establishment of precedents.

Structure and behaviour

In principle, there is a choice between using the regulation of industry structure to prevent the acquisition of market power, or using the regulation of business conduct to prevent its abuse. The effectiveness of conduct regulation is, however, limited by the need for a detailed understanding of the circumstances of each case. The regulation of industry structure may thus appear preferable, but other factors such as the advantages of large-scale operation may count against it. Regulatory systems that are concerned exclusively with the promotion of competition are likely to implement that objective mainly by stringent control upon mergers and by the breaking up of existing monopolies. Where more weight is given to the promotion of productive efficiency, account is likely to be taken of the benefits of mergers and of the costs of disruption. The more permissive attitude toward mergers which such objectives imply may require a correspondingly severe attitude toward the abuse of market power.

Predictability and effectiveness

The effectiveness of a regulatory system may depend upon how well its methodology matches the situations to which it is applied. An attempt to regulate a complex situation by means of simple form-based rules may be expected to produce erratic results, while a discretionary effects-based system may be a cumbersome way of dealing with simpler situations. Within any given system, however, the conduct of the regulatory authorities is likely to be the crucial factor. Erratic and unpredictable conduct can limit the effectiveness of the system, besides imposing unnecessary costs upon business. Conduct which conveys clear signals to businessmen can, on the other hand, bring customary business behaviour more closely into line with policy objectives, and thus reduce the need for further intervention.

The solution to the problem of how to regulate the regulators would therefore seem to depend upon a periodical review of the effects of their decisions upon the perceptions of businessmen, and of the likely consequences of those perceptions for the community as a whole.

D   The antitrust legacy

United States antitrust policy has had a strong influence upon the development of policy in Britain and in the European Union. When the present framework of competition policy was being created in post-war Britain, its legislators had before them the record of fifty years of operation of United States policy to serve as an example and a warning. Whatever its strengths and weaknesses, the American system has behind it an incomparable wealth of practical experience and analytical development. The atmosphere of political controversy which has often surrounded the subject in the United States has also served as a stimulus to its intellectual development, to an extent which is unparalleled elsewhere. Consequently, the bulk of the literature on competition policy is of American origin, and the ideas, terminology and methods of analysis which originated there are a vital part of the background to British and European thinking.

The Sherman Act and the rule of reason

The term 'antitrust' originated from the nineteenth-century practice of placing the stock of a large number of competing companies into the hands of trustees who were then able to restrict competition in that industry. Public indignation at that and other perceived abuses by big business led to the passing in 1890 of the Sherman Act. That legislation condemned such practices in stark and uncompromising terms:

> Every contract, combination in the form of trust ... or otherwise, or conspiracy in restraint of trade ... is hereby declared illegal. ... Every person who shall monopolise or attempt to monopolise ... any part of trade or commerce shall be deemed guilty of a felony.

Practices failing within either of those broad categories thus became criminal offences. Initially, however, the Act was found to be unworkable. Its form-based prohibitions were so general as to catch a wide range of established and harmless business practices. Supreme

Court interpretations eventually provided workable interpretations by introducing 'the rule of reason', under which certain forms of business behaviour could be judged, not solely by their form, but also by their effects or by the intent of the parties concerned. Nevertheless, a wide range of business practices, including price-fixing agreements, market-sharing, and refusal to supply, continue to be deemed to be illegal *per se* – so that proof of their existence is sufficient to secure a conviction, and no defence relating to their effects is allowable.

The Sherman Act was supplemented in 1914 by the more specific terms of the Clayton Act. Among practices made unlawful under that act were price discrimination, exclusive dealing, tie-in sales, and inter-locking directorates – subject in each case to the condition that the purpose or effect of the practice would be 'substantially to lessen competition'. Section 2, dealing with price discrimination, was amended in 1936 by the Robinson–Patman Act, which made it unlawful to discriminate in price between different purchasers of goods of like grade and quality where the effect would be substantially to lessen competition (unless the price differentials would only compensate for differences in costs of supply). Section 7 of the Clayton Act, as amended in 1950, prohibited mergers which would substantially lessen competition. The Clayton Act and its amendments do not create criminal offences.

Objectives and interpretations

Supreme Court interpretations have attributed objectives to the legislators of the Sherman Act, which go beyond the pursuit of economic efficiency. For example, Judge Learned Hand said that:

> great industrial consolidations are undesirable regardless of their economic results ... among the purposes of Congress in 1890 was a desire to put an end to great aggregations of capital because of the helplessness of the individual before them.[21]

and in 1962 the Supreme Court attributed to Congress the policy of 'protecting viable, small, locally owned businesses ... even at the expense of occasional higher costs and prices'.[22] The use of competition policy to attack big business and to protect small firms continued to be a feature of the US approach until appointees of the Reagan Administration took steps to limit that use of antitrust policy.

---

[21] *ALCOA 1945.*
[22] *Brown Shoe 1962.*

The actual wording of the antitrust legislation is, however, exclusively concerned with competition and, until 1977, it was interpreted to exclude consideration of offsetting gains in productive efficiency. In one merger case, the Supreme Court went so far as to rule that not only were gains in productive efficiency no defence, but that they could actually be used to attack a merger proposal since small rivals could be damaged thereby. In 1977, the Supreme Court overruled previous precedents and accepted that gains in the efficiency of distribution provided a valid defence of locational restrictions under a franchising arrangement.[23] No such defence is permitted for resale price maintenance, which therefore remains illegal.

Despite its preoccupation with practices which would give power to raise prices, the charging of excessive prices does not in itself attract disapproval under US antitrust law. In one case, indeed, the Court of Appeals ruled that excessive pricing is pro-competitive in view of the incentive it provides to new entrants.[24] In other cases the courts have shown a strong reluctance to put themselves in the position of price regulators.

The burden of proof that a merger would not harm competition falls at present upon its proponent, and the mere possibility that there might be even a very small reduction of competition has in the past been sufficient to justify prohibition. Merger guidelines issued by the Department of Justice now provide for reasonably precise criteria which take account of market shares, ease of entry and efficiency gains.

The proposals of the Chicago School

Thus, although the US antitrust system operates in principle on the basis of legal precedents, those precedents have not always presented a consistent philosophy and they have on occasion been overruled. Some of the Supreme Court's decisions have been strongly attacked by economists and lawyers of the *Chicago School* who, under the Reagan Administration, came to occupy influential positions in the Department of Justice. The Chicago School are particularly critical of judgements based upon antipathy to big business, and of those which neglected the benefits to consumers from gains in productive efficiency. They advocate a move to a wholly effects-based system in which the economic welfare of consumers would be the sole criterion. (Economic welfare in that sense is, however, interpreted narrowly to include only

[23] *Sylvania 1977.*
[24] *Berkey Photo 1979.*

effects on prices and consumer choice, and the idea of adopting a broadly defined 'public interest' criterion is firmly rejected.) Some members of the Chicago School have put forward analytical procedures for determining the trade-off between losses of allocative efficiency resulting from restrictions upon competition, and offsetting gains in productive efficiency[25]. Others[26] have argued that the task of measuring efficiency is itself impossible, and that all agreements which are 'ancillary to an integration of productive economic activity' should be permitted – including resale price maintenance

The main influence of the Chicago School upon competition policy under the Reagan administration was a strong reluctance to take action, particularly against vertical restraints. There have been signs of a reversal of that policy under the Bush and Clinton administrations.

Enforcement and effectiveness

The effectiveness of US antitrust law owes much to its methods of enforcement. A violation of the Sherman Act is a criminal offence, punishable by fines or imprisonment. Injunctions may be granted by the courts under that and other antitrust legislation, to prevent anti-competitive behaviour or to require divestiture of parts of a monopoly. Injured parties may bring actions for 'triple damages', that is to say compensation amounting to three times the amount of the damage actually sustained. Taken together with legal presumptions which often tend to go against the defendant, these are powerful deterrents.

Notwithstanding the controversy about the total economic effect of antitrust, there can be no denying its effectiveness in promoting competition. The breaking up of giant corporations such as Standard Oil and IT&T are among its more dramatic achievements, and it has undoubtedly had a pervasive effect upon business behaviour throughout the United States.

[25] For example, Williamson 1987, Chapter 1.
[26] For instance, Bork 1978 pp. 125 and 406.

2
The Legislative Framework

A Introduction

The British and European Union competition laws do no more than set a framework within which competition policy operates. They are framed in terms which are often too broad to convey to business executives more than the most general indication of what is expected of them. Their main purpose is to set up regulatory agencies, to define the limits of their operation, to provide them with broad objectives and guidelines, and to determine their procedures. What little they do have to say about business practices is nevertheless a major influence on the conduct of the regulatory authorities.

This chapter sets out their statutory objectives, and paraphrases their specific provisions concerning business structure and practices. Their provisions concerning the appointment of regulatory agencies, and their procedures are dealt with in the next chapter, and questions of interpretation are examined in Part II. It is intended here to do no more than provide a convenient index to those parts of the legislation which deal with business practices and structures, and to give a concise survey of their substance.

United Kingdom law is cited separately from European Union law under each heading, but it is emphasised that section 60 of the Competition Act 1998 requires UK courts to ensure that there is no inconsistency between the principles that they apply and the decisions that they reach, as compared with the principles laid down by the Treaty and the decisions of the European Court.

The relevant material is assembled under four headings as follows:

B Agreements
C Abuse of a dominant position

D   Mergers and joint ventures
E   Public utilities.

(EU Treaty articles are numbered as in the Treaty of Amsterdam, which was signed in 1997. The corresponding numbering of the Treaty of Rome is shown in Appendix 2 at the end of the book. Appendix 2 also indicates how to get copies of the legislation and associated guides. The technical terms used are defined in Appendix 1.)

B   Agreements

European Union law

The Treaty of Amsterdam prohibits as incompatible with the common market:

all agreements between undertakings, decisions by associations of undertakings and concerted practices which may affect trade between member states and which have as their object or effect the prevention, restriction or distortion of competition within the common market and in particular those which:

(a)   directly or indirectly fix purchase or selling prices or any other trading conditions;

(b)   limit or control production, market, technical development or investment;

(c)   share markets or sources of supply;

(d)   apply dissimilar conditions to equivalent transactions with other trading parties, thereby placing them at a competitive disadvantage;

(e)   make the conclusion of contracts subject to acceptance by the other parties of supplementary obligations which, by their nature or according to commercial usage, have no connection with the subject of such contracts.

(Article 81(3))[1]

Any such agreements are automatically void.

(Article 81(2))

Breaches of the prohibition may attract fines of up to ten per cent of turnover, and periodic penalties may be imposed for continuing breaches.

(Articles 16 & 17 of Regulation 17)

[1] Article 81 of the Treaty of Amsterdam replaced Article 85 of the Treaty of Rome in 1997.

Individual exemptions

Exemptions to the above provisions may be granted by the Commission where the practice:

contributes to improving the production or distribution of goods or to promoting technical or economic progress, while allowing consumers a fair share of the resulting benefit, and does not:

(a) impose on the undertakings concerned restrictions which are not indispensable to the attainment of those objectives;

(b) afford such undertakings the possibility of eliminating competition in respect of a substantial part of the products in question.

(Article 81(3))

Where individual exemption is required under Article 81(3), the practice must be notified to the Commission, except in the case of certain bilateral agreements relating to vertical restraints, standards, joint R&D or specialisation, and single-country practices which do not relate to trade between member states (see Annex 2.3 to this chapter).

(Regulation 17)

(The procedure for notification is described in Chapter 3.)

Block exemptions

The block exemptions listed below consist of a number of closely defined conditions under which specified practices are exempt from the provisions of Article 81(1), together with a *blacklist* of practices which can never be exempted.

- vertical restraints   (due to come into force in the year 2,000)

(see Annex 2.4)

- the distribution and servicing of motor vehicles;

(Regulation 1475/95)

- specialisation agreements;*

(Regulation 417/85)

- research and development agreements;*

(Regulation 418/84)

- insurance agreements;*

(Regulation 1534/91)

- technology transfer agreements*

(Regulation 240/96)

* (due to be superseded by the vertical restraints exemption in the year 2000)

Special exemptions have also been granted for certain agreements involving road, sea and air transport undertakings.

De minimis

The Commission has advised that agreements need not be notified if they are concerned with goods or services which do not represent more than 5 per cent of the market in the area of the common market covered by a horizontal agreement – or 10 per cent in the case of vertical agreements.

(OJ C 372 of 9/12/1997)

United Kingdom law

For agreements which may affect trade within the United Kingdom, Chapter 1 of the Competition Act 1998 stipulates the same prohibitions as Article 81 of the Treaty of Amsterdam, subject to certain exclusions and exemptions.

Exclusions

The Act specifically excludes from the prohibition certain categories of agreement:

(a) an agreement which would result in a merger or joint venture falling within the merger provisions of the Fair Trading Act 1973;[2]

(b) an agreement which is subject to competition scrutiny under other legislation;

(c) an agreement which:
   - is required in order to comply with planning obligations;
   - is the subject of a direction under section 21(2) of the Restrictive Trade Practices Act 1976;
   - forms the constitution of a market regulated by a European Economic Area;
   - relates to the operation of services of 'general economic interest' or of a 'revenue-producing monopoly';
   - is necessary to comply with a specified legal requirement;
   - is necessary to avoid conflict with international treaty obligations;
   - relates to a market which falls within the coal and steel provisions of the Treaty of Paris, or where it relates to production of or trade in 'agricultural products' as defined in the Treaty and in

---

[2] The exclusion may be withdrawn under the circumstances described in OFT Guide 416 *Exclusion for Mergers and Ancillary Restrictions*.

Council Regulation (EEC) No. 26/62, or to farmers' cooperatives; or
- where there are overriding national policy considerations,
- an agreement which involves the rules regulating a professional service;

(d)   rules of professional bodies as designated in Schedule 4 of the Act;
(e)   vertical agreements, except where otherwise stipulated by the Director-General.

The Secretary of State has the power to add, amend or remove exclusions in certain circumstances.

(s3 of the Competition Act 1998)

Exemptions

Individual exemptions may be granted under the same conditions as under Article 81(3) above.

Block exemptions cover particular classes of agreements which are beneficial under the same criteria, or which are of minor significance, or which have no adverse effect on competition. An agreement which falls within a block exemption need not be notified.

Parallel exemptions apply to agreements with individual or block exemption under Article 81(3) of the Treaty of Amsterdam, which are automatically exempt under the UK legislation. They also cover agreements which fall within the terms of an EC block exemption but which are not subject to Article 81 because they do not affect inter-state trade. Agreements covered by a parallel exemption need not be notified to the Director-General. The Director-General may, however, vary or remove the exemption in certain specified circumstances. Exemptions are time-limited and may be granted subject to certain specified conditions.

Exempt agreements are legally enforceable unless other legislation makes them unenforceable, and they are not open to third-party action or penalty.

(s4 of the Competition Act 1998)

De minimis

Agreements which do not have an appreciable effect on competition need not be notified to the Director-General. An agreement will be in that category if the market share of the parties is no more 10 per cent, and is likely to be if it is less than 25 per cent, unless – in either case – they are price-fixing or market-sharing agreements or part of a network of agreements.

C   Abuse of a dominant position

European Union law

The Treaty of Amsterdam prohibits as incompatible with the common market:

> any abuse by one or more undertakings of a dominant position[3] within the common market or in a substantial part of it... in so far as it may affect trade between member states. Such abuse may in particular consist in:
> - (a)   directly or indirectly imposing unfair purchase or selling prices or unfair trading conditions;
> - (b)   limiting production, markets or technical development to the prejudice of consumers;
> - (c)   applying dissimilar conditions to equivalent transactions with other trading parties, thereby placing them at a competitive disadvantage;
> - (d)   making the conclusion of contracts subject to acceptance by the other parties of supplementary obligations which, by their nature or according to commercial usage, have no connection with the subject of such contracts.

(Article 82)[4]

United Kingdom law

For conduct which may affect trade within the United Kingdom, chapter II of the Competition Act 1998 stipulates the same prohibitions as Article 82 of the Treaty of Amsterdam, subject to certain exclusions.

Exclusions

There are specific exclusions for:
- behaviour which results in a merger or joint venture within the meaning of the Fair Trading Act 1973;
- undertakings entrusted with the operation of 'services of general economic interest' or a revenue-producing monopoly';
- behaviour engaged in order to comply with a legal requirement;
- avoidance of conflict with international obligations;

---

[3] The interpretation of the term *dominant position* is discussed in section C of Chapter 4.

[4] Article 82 of the Treaty of Amsterdam replaced Article 86 of the Treaty of Rome in 1997.

– behaviour which relates to a coal or steel product as listed in the European Coal and Steel Treaty.

The Secretary of State has the power to add, amend or remove exclusions in certain circumstances.

(s19 of the Competition Act 1998)

Monopoly references

Where the prohibitions of the Competition Act have been infringed and where abuse continues despite enforcement action, and a *monopoly situation*[5] exists, the Director-General may make a reference to the Competition Commission. Also, a reference may be made if a group of businesses constituting a *complex monopoly*[5] all adopt similar practices which appear to be anti-competitive, but where there is no suggestion that they are colluding or acting in concert. If the Competition Commission then finds that an act or omission on the part of those concerned may be expected to operate against the public interest[6] the Secretary of State may use his powers under the Fair Trading Act to impose a remedy.

D   Mergers and joint ventures

(The interpretation of the legislation summarised below is discussed in Chapter 5.)

European Union law

The merger regulation requires that:

> A concentration which creates or strengthens a *dominant position*[7] as a result of which effective competition would be significantly impeded in the common market or in a substantial part of it shall be declared incompatible with the common market.

A *concentration* is deemed to arise where:

(a) two or more previously independent undertakings merge, or
(b) one or more persons already controlling at least one undertaking, or one or more undertakings:
     acquire, whether by purchase of securities or assets, by contract or

---

[5] Defined in Annex 2.2 below.
[6] Defined in Annex 2.2. below.
[7] See section C of Chapter 4.

by other means direct or indirect control of the whole or parts of one or more other undertakings.

A joint venture is, however, deemed to create a concentration only if it performs on a lasting basis all the functions of an autonomous economic entity and has all the necessary resources to perform those functions, in terms of funding, staff and tangible and intangible assets. Such a joint venture is termed *full-function*.[8]

A concentration having a *community dimension* must be notified to the Commission and will be prohibited if, in the Commission's opinion it is, for the above reason, incompatible with the common market.

Concentrations having a community dimension are those meeting the following criteria:

(a) the companies concerned have a combined worldwide turnover greater than 2.5 billion ecu;

(b) at least two of the companies concerned have a Community wide turnover greater than 100 million ecu;

(c) in each of three member states the aggregate turnover of each of at least two of the undertakings concerned is greater than 25 million ecu; and,

(d) the community-wide turnover of at least two of the undertakings concerned is greater than 100 million ecu.

The general intention is that no merger should fall within the jurisdictions both of the Community and of a member state.[9]

Regulation 4064/89[10]

United Kingdom law

A *merger situation* qualifying for investigation is taken to occur if:

(a) two or more enterprises *cease to be distinct enterprises* (see below), or there are arrangements in progress which will lead to enterprises ceasing to be distinct;

(b) at least one of which was carried on in the United Kingdom or under the control of a body corporate incorporated in the United Kingdom;

---

[8] Interpretation of the term *full-function* is discussed on p. 87.
[9] Notice on Cooperation between National Authorities and the Commission OJC 313 15/10/97.
[10] As amended by Council Regulation (EC) 1310/97 of 30/6/97 OJ L 180 9/7/97 & OJ L40 13/2/98.

(c)   either the merger has not yet taken place or it has taken place not more than four months before the reference is made, unless it took place without public notice and without the Secretary of State or the Director-General being told about it (in which case the four-month period starts from the announcement or the time the Secretary of State or the Director-General is told); and

(d)   either:
- those enterprises would together supply or receive at least one-quarter of the goods or services of a particular description supplied in the United Kingdom or a substantial part of it; or,
- the value of the assets[11] taken over exceeds £70 million.

(Section 64 FTA)

Enterprises are taken to cease to be distinct enterprises if either:

(a)   they are brought under common ownership or *common control* (see below) – whether or not the business to which either of them formerly belonged continues to be carried on under the same or different ownership or control – or,

(b)   either of the enterprises ceases to be carried on at all and does so in consequence of any arrangements or transaction entered into to prevent competition between the enterprises.

Enterprises are taken to be under 'common control' if they are:

(a)   enterprises of interconnected bodies corporate; or,

(b)   enterprises carried on by two or more bodies corporate of which one and the same person or group of persons *has control* (see below); or,

(c)   an enterprise carried on by a body corporate and an enterprise carried on by a person or group of persons having control of that body corporate.

A person is regarded as 'having control' of an enterprise if he is able directly or indirectly materially to influence[12] the policy of that enterprise, although not having a controlling interest in it.

(Section 65 FTA)

If as a result of a reference to the Monopolies and Mergers Commission, a merger situation qualifying for investigation is found to exist and it is found that it operates or may be expected to operate against the *public*

---

[11] Current and fixed assets plus investments less provisions for depreciation, and so on – see OFT Guide (Appendix 2).

[12] The degree of influence required is discussed on p. 80.

interest[13] the Secretary of State is empowered to take action to remedy or prevent any adverse effects specified in the Commission's report.

(Section 73 FTA)

There are also special provisions concerning newspaper mergers.

(Sections 57–62 FTA)

Parties to a merger referred to the Commission may not acquire each other's shares without the permission of the Secretary of State.

(Companies Act 1989)

E   Public utilities

European Union law

The conduct of governments towards state enterprises and public utilities is regulated under the Treaty of Amsterdam as follows:

> In the case of public undertakings and undertakings to which member states grant special or exclusive rights, member states shall neither enact nor maintain in force any measure contrary to the rules contained in this Treaty, in particular those provided for in ... Articles 81 to 90.

(Article 86 (1))

The conduct of such undertakings is regulated as follows:

> Undertakings entrusted with the operation of services of general economic interest or having the character of a revenue-producing monopoly shall be subject to the rules contained in this Treaty, in particular to the rules on competition, in so far as the application of such rules does not obstruct the performance, in law or in fact of the particular tasks assigned to them. The development of trade must not be affected to such an extent as would be contrary to the interests of the Community.

(Article 86(2))

United Kingdom law

Public sector references

References may be made by the Secretary of State to the Competition Commission concerning:

(a)   the efficiency and costs of,

[13] The term *the public interest* is defined on p. 30.

(b)   the service provided by, or

(c)   possible abuse of a monopoly situation by,

any body corporate which supplies goods or services by way of business, whose controlling members are appointed by a minister.

(Section 11 of the Competition Act 1980)

If the Commission finds that the public sector body in question is pursuing a course of conduct which is against the public interest the responsible minister is empowered to order appropriate remedies.

Other public utilities

The provisions of Chapters 1 and 2 of the Competition Act 1998 apply to the public utilities, and the Act enables the Regulators appointed under the various privatisation acts to exercise, concurrently with the Director-General of Fair Trading, most of the functions of the Director-General of Fair Trading under that Act.[14] Disputes concerning price-regulation and other aspects of the regulation of the privatised utilities' licences may be referred to the Competition Commission for adjudication.

Annex 2.1:   The public interest

The public interest is defined in s84 of the Fair Trading Act 1973 in the following terms:

> In determining whether any particular matter operates, or may be expected to operate, against the public interest, the Commission shall take into account all matters which appear to them in the particular circumstances to be relevant and, among other things, shall have regard to the desirability
>
> (a)   of maintaining and promoting effective competition between persons supplying goods and services in the United Kingdom;
>
> (b)   of promoting the interests of consumers, purchasers and other users of goods and services in the United Kingdom in respect of the prices charged for them and in respect of their quality and the variety of goods and services supplied;
>
> (c)   of promoting, through competition, the reduction of costs and the development and use of new techniques and new products, and of facilitating the entry of new competitors into existing markets;

---

[14] See OFT guide *The Competition Act 1998: Concurrent Application to the Regulated Industries* (see Appendix 2 for contact).

(d) of maintaining and promoting the balanced distribution of industry and employment in the United Kingdom; and

(e) of maintaining and promoting competitive activity in markets outside the United Kingdom on the part of producers of goods and of suppliers of goods and services, in the United Kingdom.

Annex 2.2: Definitions of 'monopoly situation' and 'complex monopoly'

The Fair Trading Act 1973 provides for inquiries to determine whether a statutory 'monopoly situation' or 'complex monopoly' exists and if so whether any act or omission on the part of those concerned operates or may be expected to operate against the public interest.

Definition of a 'monopoly situation'

A monopoly situation in relation to the supply of goods is taken to exist if:

(a) at least one-quarter of all the goods of any description which are supplied in the United Kingdom are supplied by one and the same person, or are supplied to one and the same person; or

(b) at least one-quarter of all the goods of any description which are supplied in the United Kingdom are supplied by members of one and the same group of interconnected bodies corporate, or are supplied to members of one and the same group of interconnected bodies corporate; or

(c) at least one-quarter of all the goods of any description which are supplied in the United Kingdom are supplied by members of one and the same group constituting a 'complex monopoly' (as defined below) or are supplied to members of one and the same such group; or

(d) one or more agreements are in operation, the result of which is that goods of any description are not supplied in the United Kingdom at all.

(Section 6(1) FTA)

A monopoly situation is taken to exist in relation to the exports of goods of any description if:

(a) at least one quarter of the goods of that description are produced by a person or by members of a group as defined in (a) or (b) above (in which case the monopoly situation is taken to exist both for exports of goods of that description from the United Kingdom generally and for the exports of those goods to each market taken separately); or,

(b) there are agreements in operation, concerning at least one quarter of those goods which are produced in the United Kingdom, which in any way prevent restrict or distort competition in export markets.

(Section 8 FTA)

A monopoly situation in relation to the supply of services in the United Kingdom is defined in the same terms as for the supply of goods above, except that services may be treated as supplied in the United Kingdom if the supplier:

(a) has a place of business in the United Kingdom, or
(b) controls the relevant activities from the United Kingdom, or
(c) being a body corporate, is incorporated under the law of Great Britain or of Northern Ireland.

(Section 7 FTA)

Definition of a 'complex monopoly'

A complex monopoly is taken to exist if the members of the group referred to in (c) above, so conduct their affairs – whether voluntarily or not, and whether by agreement or not – as in any way to prevent, restrict or distort competition in connection with the production of goods or the supply of services, whether or not they themselves are affected by the competition and whether the competition is between persons interested as producers or suppliers or between persons interested as customers of producers or suppliers.

(Sections 6(2) & 7(2) FTA)

Annex 2.3:   Exemptions from notification of agreements for Article 81 (3)

(Extract from Regulation 17)

Notification of new agreements, decisions and practices

1. Agreements, decisions and concerted practices of the kind described in Article 81(1) of the Treaty which come into existence after the entry into force of this Regulation and in respect of which the parties seek application of Article 81(3) must be

notified to the Commission. Until they have been notified, no decision in application of Article 81(3) may be taken.

2. Paragraph 1 shall not apply to agreements, decisions or concerted practices where:

    (1) the only parties thereto are undertakings from one Member State and the agreements, decisions or practices do not relate either to imports or to exports between Member States;

    (2) not more than two undertakings are party thereto, and the agreements only:

        (a) restrict the freedom of one party to the contract in determining the prices or conditions of business upon which the goods which he has obtained from the other party to the contract may be resold; or

        (b) impose restrictions on the exercise of the rights of the assignee or user of industrial property rights – in particular patents, utility models, designs or trade marks – or of the person entitled under a contract to the assignment, or grant, of the right to use a method of manufacture or knowledge relating to the use and to the application of industrial processes;

    (3) they have as their sole object:

        (a) the development or uniform application of standards or types; or

        (b) joint research and development;

        (c) specialisation in the manufacture of products, including agreements necessary for achieving this

            • where the products which are the subject of specialisation do not, in a substantial part of the common market, represent more than 15 per cent of the volume of business done in identical products or those considered by the consumers to be similar by reason of their characteristics, price and use, and

            • where the total annual turnover of the participating undertakings does not exceed 200 million units of account.

These agreements, decisions and concerted practices may be notified to the Commission.

Annex 2.4: The vertical restraints block exemption

The block exemption is due to be published in the course of 1999 and will then be available on the European Commission's website (see Appendix 2 at the end of the book).

On the basis of proposals by DGIV in January 1999, it appears probable that there will be the following exclusions.

The block exemption would not apply to vertical restraints which directly or indirectly, in isolation or in combination with other factors under control of the parties including the exercise of industrial property rights, have the following object or effect:

(1) resale price maintenance, except maximum resale prices or recommended resale prices provided that these do not amount to fixed or minimum resale prices as a result of pressure or incentives created by any of parties;

(2) the prevention or restriction of imports or exports, except restrictions on active sales outside or into an allocated territory;

(3) the prevention or restriction of passive sales, except restrictions on sales to unauthorised distributors by the members of a selective distribution system and restrictions on the use by the buyer of intermediate goods and/or services which are supplied for incorporation;

(4) the combination, at the same level of distribution, of selective distribution and exclusive distribution containing a prohibition or restriction on active selling;

(5) the prevention or restriction of cross-supplies between distributions within a selective distribution system;

(6) an obligation on the supplier of an intermediate good or service not to sell the same good or service as a repair or replacement good or service to the independent aftermarket.

In a statement to the Industrial Affairs Council on 29 April 1999,[15] the Commission stated that it had in mind a market share threshold of 30 per cent, above which the exemption would not apply.

[15] Press Notice IP/99/286 7/5/99.

3
Regulatory Institutions and Procedures

A Introduction

The definitions of business practices which appear in European Union and United Kingdom legislation are framed in very general terms. Application of the legislation to individual cases consequently requires the exercise of discretion going far beyond that normally required of ordinary courts of law. The legislation accordingly made provision for the creation of special institutions which were given the duty to exercise such discretion within prescribed limits and according to stated procedures. Since the legislation was first introduced, those regulatory institutions have developed further procedures and practices of their own, and have at times assumed roles which were not specifically catered for in the legislation. This chapter concentrates upon those aspects of law and practice which appear significantly to affect the conduct of the business of the regulatory authorities.

The European Commission has sought to build a comprehensive body of compliance rules and precedents with the express aim of influencing business conduct. That appears also to be the current intention of the UK authorities. The normal practice of the former Monopolies and Mergers Commission, on the other hand, was to base each judgement exclusively upon the direct consequences of the case before them, without explicit regard to its effect upon wider business conduct. While their judgements do, for the most part, present a readily discernible pattern, there have been a few exceptions which – for a time at least – faced businesses with some uncertainty.

The dominant influence upon the conduct of the regulatory bodies has, however, been the quantity and quality of the human resources at their disposal. Those bodies are very small compared with the typical organisation which they are required to regulate, and the rewards and career prospects which they offer are also generally inferior. Resource constraints thus tend to limit the initiatives that they can take, and their responses to the demands made upon them. One consequence is that the majority of their work has had to be performed informally. Another is that, under pressure of work, their procedures and analytical methods may sometimes have been abbreviated or performed summarily.

The remainder of this chapter summarises the constitution, powers and procedures of each of the following institutions:

B The European Union
C The Office of Fair Trading
D The Competition Commission
E The Secretary of State
F The courts.

B   The European Union

The competition rules and policies of the European Union apply throughout the European Economic Area, but the institutions and procedures described below apply only where trade with members of the EU is likely to be affected. The national authorities of member states may apply the prohibitions laid down in Articles 81 and 82 in their national courts,[1] and this provision has been implemented in some EU countries. Individuals in member countries may also apply to their national courts for judgements under Articles 81 and 82. In practice, however, little use has been made of the national courts for that purpose, and the implementation of EU competition law has fallen almost entirely to the European Commission and the European Courts of Justice.

EU competition policy institutions[2]

The Commission

The European Commission is given a central role in competition policy by Article 85 of the Treaty of Amsterdam:[3]

the Commission shall . . . ensure the application of the principles laid down in Articles 81 and 82. On application by a member state or on

[1] As provided for in Regulation 17, Art 9(3).
[2] For a more detailed account of the institutions and procedures, see Cini and McGowan 1998.
[3] Originally Article 89 of the Treaty of Rome.

its own initiative, and in cooperation with the competent authorities in the member states, who shall give it their assistance, the Commission shall investigate cases of suspected infringement of these principles. If it finds that there has been an infringement, it shall propose appropriate measures to bring it to an end. If the infringement is not brought to an end, the Commission shall record such an infringement in a reasoned decision. The Commission may publish its decision and authorise member states to take the measures, the conditions and details of which it shall determine, needed to remedy the situation.

Commission decisions are taken collectively by the College of Commissioners which consists of 20 Commissioners appointed by member governments. The Commission is responsible for executing the policy decisions of the Council of Ministers but in respect of individual cases under Articles 81 and 82, it can take legally binding decisions without reference to the Council.

The Commissioners are supported by a Secretariat and by the Legal Service, which reports directly to the President of the Commission. The Legal Service advises on the legality of Commission decisions, and represents the Commission in the Court of Justice. The executive work of the Commission is done by some 24 Directorates-General, each of which is the special responsibility of one of the Commissioners.

The Directorate-General for Competition (DGIV) is divided into seven directorates:

A Coordination and policy
B Mergers
C, D, E and F Concerted practices and abuse of a dominant position (the different directorates being responsible for different markets); and
G State aids;

to which has recently been added the Anti-Cartel Unit.

Case officers or rapporteurs take responsibility for individual cases, for which they undertake economic and legal analyses, draft decisions and monitor compliance.

The roles of other EU institutions

The role of the Commission in other spheres is usually to formulate proposals for decision by the Council of Ministers but in the day-to-day execution of competition policy, the Commission makes its own decisions. The roles of other Community institutions which have duties relating to competition policy are:

(a) The Council of Ministers

The Council consists of one representative from the government of each member state. The Council has the power, acting by a qualified majority, and after consulting the European Parliament, to adopt appropriate regulations or directives proposed by the Commission to give effect to the principles set out in Articles 81 and 82 of the Treaty.

(b) The European Parliament

The Parliament has powers to guide and supervise the Commission. It makes an annual appraisal of the Commission's competition policy activities, expressed in the form of a resolution on the Commission's report on competition policy, and advises the Council on the Commission's legislative proposals. Similar functions are also performed by the separate Economic and Social Committee.

(c) The Court of First Instance

The Court consists of 15 members, any one of whom may be called upon to act in a specific case as an advocate-general. It has jurisdiction in actions brought against the Commission or the Council on the grounds of lack of competence, infringement of an essential procedural requirement, infringement of the Treaty or of its rules of application, or misuse of powers. The Court also has the power to review and alter penalties imposed by the Commission. The Court rules only on legally binding decisions, and does not normally consider procedural irregularities unless they could affect such decisions.

It is the duty of the Court to enforce the treaty requirement that all decisions must be reasoned.[4] In appeals against a decision of the Commission that there has been an infringement of the Treaty, the burden of proof lies with the Commission. Thus, although in principle the Court is concerned with matters of procedure rather than of substance, it may annul a Commission decision on the grounds of error of material fact, inadequacy of reasoning or lack of adequate proof. In practice, therefore, it can become involved in the analytical merits of the Commission's arguments on matter of substance.

---

[4] Art. 190 of the Treaty of Rome.

(d)   The Court of Justice of the European Union

The Court of Justice consists of 15 judges assisted by a number of Advocates-General.[5] It hears appeals against decisions of the Court of First Instance. The Court may also give preliminary rulings on matters raised in the courts of member states which bear upon the interpretation of the Treaty, or of Community legislation, or upon the validity of decisions of the Commission or of the Council. A national court may apply for such a ruling where it appears necessary to enable it to give judgement. Where such a question is raised in a case before a national court, against whose decisions there is no remedy under national law (i.e. if it is a court of final appeal), that court is required to refer the matter to the Court of Justice.

The Court's procedure normally consists of the examination of written evidence, followed by a brief oral hearing. There is no provision for dissenting judgements.

(e) & (f)   The Advisory Committee for Restrictive Practices and Mono- polies and the Advisory Committee for Concentrations.

These committees comprise experts appointed by each of the mem- ber states. The appropriate committee is consulted by DGIV before referring a proposed decision to the Commission.

The procedures of the EU Commission[6]

Conduct prohibited by Articles 81 or 82 is illegal even if there has been no official decision to that effect. To obtain legal immunity from prohibitions and penalties for agreements, it is necessary[7] to follow the formal procedure of notification. An agreement for which a formal exemption is granted remains legally valid for the period of the exemp- tion.

Notification

Notification is a procedure by which an agreement falling within Article 81(1) of the Treaty can be granted an exemption.[8] However, under

---

[5] Of the same status as the judges; they deliver an opinion to the judges before the latter make a decision.

[6] Regulation 17 (JO 1962, 204; OJ Spec.Ed 1959–1952, 87) is the legal basis for these procedures, which, however, are due for extensive revision according to Commission proposals in their 1999 White Paper (Commission programme No. 99/027).

[7] Except for agreements covered by a block exemption.

[8] As provided for in Article 81(3) – see section B of Chapter 2 above – and Article 9(1) of Regulation 17.

Article 4(2) of Regulation 17, notification of an agreement is not necessary for that purpose in the case of agreements within one member state which do not affect trade between member states. There is no legal requirement to notify an agreement, but notification confers interim immunity from penalties, and enables the agreement to be given retrospective legal validity if exemption is obtained.[9]

Application for negative clearance

Application for negative clearance is a procedure for seeking a declaration that a practice falls outside the scope of Article 81(1) and/or Article 82 of the Treaty. It is normal practice to submit such an application at the same time as a notification, and on the same form.[10] Unlike notification, application does not confer interim immunity from penalties.

On receipt of a notification or application, the Commission may seek further information from applicants or from third parties, and may suggest amendments to the arrangements that may make them acceptable.

Individual exemptions

In response to a notification, the Commission may exempt an agreement from the prohibition of Article 81(1) on the grounds that it meets the requirements of Article 81(3). The Commission may require the agreement to be amended before doing so, or it may make exemption subject to stated conditions. Exemptions are reported in the *Official Journal*. However, it is more usual for the Commission to issue a comfort letter (see below). There can be no exemption from the prohibition of Article 82.

Block exemptions

Regulations are issued from time to time, conferring conditional exemption on defined groups of agreements, as noted in section B of Chapter 2. Such block exemptions[11] are for a limited duration, and the Commission can withdraw the exemption from any particular agreement to which it takes exception. Compliance with a block exemption from Article 81(1) does not necessarily confer immunity from Article 82 (*Tetra Pak 1991*).

---

[9] This aspect of notification – and others – are under review.
[10] Form A/B.
[11] There is a list of block exemptions in section B of Chapter 2 (p. 22).

Opposition procedures

The regulations governing some of the block exemptions provide for an opposition procedure. This enables some classes of agreement which are not specifically exempted by a regulation to be deemed exempt if they have been notified and the Commission raises no objection within a specified time (normally six months).

Negative clearance

Negative clearance is a statement of the Commission's opinion, and it is not, strictly speaking, a legally binding decision. Before giving clearance, the Commission must publish a summary and invite comment from third parties. It must also consult the Advisory Committee on Restrictive Practices. Negative clearance remains in force unless or until it is revised in the light of a change in circumstances.

Comfort letters

As an alternative to granting formal exemption or negative clearance, the Commission may send the parties a comfort letter indicating that it has closed its file on the matter, because it sees no need to take any further action. Most applications and notifications are in fact dealt with in this way. In some cases, the Commission first publishes a summary and invites comments, as it does before making a formal decision. A comfort letter is not legally binding on the Commission, but it is likely to have a strong effect on any subsequent decision. A comfort letter can sometimes be obtained in a matter of months, as compared with periods of 18 months, or often much longer, in the case of a formal decision. Where it sees obstacles to the granting of negative clearance the Commission may issue a warning letter, explaining its concerns and giving companies the opportunity to offer undertakings or to present a defence.

Advisory notices

Articles 81 and 82 of the Treaty could be interpreted to prohibit any of a very wide range of business practices, many of which might alternatively be regarded as harmless. An important function of the Commission is therefore to let businessmen know how to conform to community legislation. Advisory notices on particular topics are issued from time to time, and much of the Commission's work is done informally in response to requests for advice. It is probable that a major consequence of the Commission's advisory activities has been the modification or abandonment of practices which might otherwise have attracted prohibitions and penalties. Advice obtained in that way is not, however, binding upon the Commission.

Merger regulation

Every qualifying merger[12] must be notified[13] to the Commission by the acquirer, if it is to be an acquisition; or otherwise jointly by the merging parties. Notification of a merger is linked to its automatic suspension for an initial period of three weeks, which may be extended. The Commission adopts a two-stage procedure:

- phase 1, which may last for up to one month, in which the Commission decides whether to permit the merger or to initiate a detailed phase 2 investigation, and during which undertakings[14] may be offered and remedies may be agreed;
- phase 2, lasting up to a further four months, during which oral hearings are held and the Advisory Committee on Concentrations is consulted.

The Commission may, under some circumstances, refer a case to the competition authorities of a member state.[15]

Powers of investigation

Something like 90 per cent of cases dealt with by the Commission are in response to applications and notifications, and the bulk of those cases are settled informally. The Commission also has a (rarely used) power to conduct a general inquiry[16] into any economic sector in which it believes that competition is being restricted or distorted within the Common Market. The remaining cases arise from the investigation of complaints and from initiatives taken as a result of the Commission's own monitoring activities.

Requests for information for the purposes of such inquiries follow the two-stage procedure:[17]

(a) a written request for information, stating the purpose of the inquiry and its legal basis, which is copied to the Office of Fair Trading;

---

[12] See section D in Chapter 2 above.
[13] The information to be included in a notification is set out in Regulation 3384/94.
[14] Usually to divest overlapping activities.
[15] See section B in Chapter 5 below.
[16] Regulation 17, Art. 12.
[17] Described in full in Regulation 17, Art. 11.

(b)   if the required information is not fully supplied within the stated time limit, a further request based upon a formal Commission decision, stipulating in detail what information is required.

Failure to supply all of the information requested may then attract a fine and a daily penalty.

There are powers to enter premises and examine business records.[18] A Commission official may demand entry – if necessary without warning – on production of a written authorisation indicating the purpose and subject matter of the investigation. An official of the Office of Fair Trading will normally accompany him. There is no right of forcible entry, but the Commission may obtain an order from the High Court requiring admission. Business records may be copied but not removed, and oral explanations may be asked for.

The Commission's powers to obtain information do not apply to privileged information such as is exchanged between a lawyer and his client, and there are strict procedures[19] governing the disclosure of confidential information provided to the Commission.

DGIV's formal procedures

If the results of an investigation indicate that there has been a breach of the competition rules, the DGIV will usually try to put an end to that breach by meetings or correspondence with those concerned. Alternatively, or if that fails, the following procedure[20] is adopted in full:

(a)   a formal Statement of Objections, briefly setting out the relevant facts, the supporting evidence and the proposed legal findings, is sent to the parties concerned, together with copies of other relevant documents;

(b)   the parties concerned are given access to the relevant Commission files to enable them to make use of other documents in their defence;

(c)   the parties concerned, and other interested parties, may make written submissions[21] within a stipulated time limit;

(d)   the applicant is given a non-confidential version of any objections and a time limit for responding:

(e)   at the request of the parties concerned or of other interested parties, there may be an oral hearing, as described below;

[18]   Regulation 17, Art. 14.
[19]   See Annex 3.1 below.
[20]   Procedures and time limits are set out in Regulations 2367/90 and 3384/94.
[21]   For which there are confidentiality provisions to protect business secrets.

(f)   DGIV consults the Advisory Committee on Restrictive Practices (or, in merger cases, the Advisory Committee on Concentrations);

(g)   The Competition Commissioner makes a recommendation to his fellow commissioners, and the Commission makes and publishes its decision.

Hearings[22] are organised and chaired by the Hearing Officer[23] whose duty it is to protect the rights of the defence. Apart from the representatives of the parties concerned, those attending may include representatives of member states and other interested parties. Proceedings are opened by a brief statement by a Commission official. The parties then make their presentations, and other witnesses may be heard. The parties may then be questioned by representatives of the Commission or of member states. Tape-recordings of the proceedings are made. The procedure throughout is intended to be administrative rather than adversarial or judicial. Hearings are held in private and do not usually last more than a day. Formal merger procedures are generally similar, but their operation is governed by strict time-limits.

Remedies and penalties

Infringements which are revealed by the above procedures are often remedied by voluntary action by the parties concerned. Remedies which may be ordered by the Commission include:

(a)   an order to terminate an agreement or practice;

(b)   an order to take positive action (for instance, to resume supplies which have been withheld);

(c)   an order requiring a company to divest itself of a company which it had acquired.

The Commission is also empowered to impose fines and periodic penalty payments on undertakings which intentionally or negligently infringe Article 81(1) or Article 82 of the Treaty. Infringements which lead to the imposition of fines are not regarded as criminal offences, but it has been established that they may be used as a general deterrent to other undertakings. Fines may range from one thousand to a maximum of one million ecu or 10 per cent of turnover, whichever is the greater.

---

[22] See Commission Regulation (EC) No 2842/98 of 22 December 1998 on hearings procedures.

[23] See the Commission notice on The Terms of Reference of the Hearing Officer OJ 1994 L330/67 [1995] or par. 201 of Comp Report 23 (1993).

Appeals. An appeal against a decision or a fine may be made to the European Court of First Instance by the parties to whom a decision is addressed or by third parties who are directly affected.

C The Office of Fair Trading

The role of the Director-General

Duties

The Director-General of Fair Trading occupies a focal position in competition policy in Britain. His powers and duties enable him:

(a) to grant individual exemptions and to make recommendations to the Secretary of State concerning block exemptions to Chapter 1 of the Competition Act 1998;

(b) to conduct investigations when there are reasonable grounds for suspecting that the prohibitions of either Chapter I or Chapter II of that Act have been infringed;

(c) to give guidance and to make decisions as to whether the prohibitions of either chapter have been infringed;

(d) to issue directions in order to put an end to such infringements and to seek enforcement of his directions in the courts;

(e) to levy penalties for intentional or negligent infringements;

(f) to collect and collate information concerning commercial activities in the United Kingdom and to monitor possible monopoly or merger situations or uncompetitive practices which may adversely affect the economic interests of consumers; and to advise the Secretary of State for Trade and Industry concerning appropriate remedial action;

(g) in particular, to advise the Secretary of State whether to make a merger reference to the Competition Commission;

(h) to advise the Secretary of State concerning the feasibility of remedies proposed by the Competition Commission;

(i) to examine the rules of certain regulatory agencies and to report to the Secretary of State concerning their effects on competition.

The Director-General also has extensive statutory duties in the field of consumer protection, including duties in connection with the codes of practice of trade associations.

The Independence of the Director-General

The Director-General is appointed by the Secretary of State for Trade and Industry, but he enjoys a considerable degree of independence.

The Secretary of State may give him general directions concerning the conduct of his duties, but those powers can only be exercised publicly, and they have seldom been used. The Secretary of State is free to ignore the Director-General's advice concerning merger references, and the legislation does not require him to reveal what advice he has been given, nor to give reasons for rejecting it. As regards individual cases, the Director-General enjoys almost total independence, but he cannot act independently on matters of competition policy. Although he has a strong influence upon the development of policy in his role as adviser to the Secretary of State, the final decisions on policy matters inevitably rest with the Secretary of State. The Director-General is not a civil servant, but on matters of general policy, his standing is similar to that of a Permanent Secretary. He is bound to give effect to any publicly announced changes of government policy, and it must be assumed that he also takes account of unpublished expressions of the Secretary of State's wishes. A former Director-General has explained that if he did not

> follow broadly the declared Government policy there would be, or there might be, a great deal of difference of view and businesspersons would not know quite where they were.   (Borrie, 1991)

Procedures

Agreements and the abuse of a dominant position[24]

Notification. There is no statutory requirement to notify an agreement and it is for the parties concerned to consider whether it might breach the prohibition. Any agreement (or practice) for which individual exemption or negative clearance is sought must, however, be notified to the Director-General. An agreement (or practice) may, however, be notified in order to obtain guidance as to whether it would fall within the prohibition, and whether it would be given individual exemption. Such guidance is not legally binding but the Director-General cannot reopen a case unless circumstances change or a complaint is received from a third party. The guidance provides immunity from penalties, but it is given in confidence without consulting third parties.

Notification has the immediate effect of rendering the notifier immune to financial penalty in respect of that agreement from the time a valid notification is received by the Director-General.

[24] See OFT guide, *Competition Act 1998: Draft Procedural Rules* (see Appendix 2 for source).

Administrative letters

An administrative letter from the Director-General has the same effect as a comfort letter from the European Commission, and it is the means of dealing with the majority of notifications.

Decisions

A decision is a reasoned statement of the Director-General's formal ruling. It may prohibit an agreement (or practice), grant it negative clearance, or give it individual exemption.[25] Before issuing a decision the Director-General invites comments from third parties. If he contemplates a prohibition, he sends those concerned a comprehensive statement of objection, to which he invites a written response and, possibly, attendance at a meeting.

Interim measures

The Director-General has the power to order the suspension of a practice or the preservation of the *status quo* while the investigation progresses. An interim measures direction may be given when he considers there to be a reasonable suspicion of infringement, and an urgent need for corrective action. Before he gives such a direction, the Director-General gives notice of what he proposes to those concerned, and invites their comments. His direction can remain in force until the investigation is completed.

Powers of investigation

The Director-General has powers of investigation[26] that are similar to those of the European Commission. Where he has reasonable grounds for suspecting an infringement of the prohibitions, he, or an officer authorised by him and acting on his behalf, can:

- require the production of any specified document, at a time or place and in the manner or form specified; take copies of any such documents, and require an explanation of the documents;
- having given at least two days' notice, enter and search premises, take copies of documents, and require explanations of documents, and require any information held in a computer to be produced in a form in which it can be taken away. Notice is not required in certain specified circumstances;

[25] See Section B in Chapter 2 above.
[26] See OFT guide, *Competition Act 1998: Investigation and Enforcement Procedures* (see Appendix 2 for source).

- enter premises without notice and using such force as is reasonably necessary, on authority of a High Court or Court of Session warrant, if he has reasonable grounds for suspecting that the premises contain documents which:
  - had previously been called for and which had not been produced;
  - would be concealed, removed, tampered with or destroyed if called for; or
  - could not be found because entry to the premises had been prevented.

The Director-General's powers to obtain information do not, however, apply to privileged information such as is exchanged between a lawyer and his client and there are strict procedures governing the disclosure of information.[27]

Obstructing the right of entry, or deliberately supplying false or misleading information to the Director-General or the appeals body, is a criminal offence.

Powers of enforcement[28]

Where he is satisfied that a breach of a prohibition has occurred, the Director-General may give a direction to those concerned to modify or put an end to the agreement and not to enter into similar agreements, or to modify or put a stop to the abusive conduct. Failure to comply with such an order leaves those concerned exposed to action for damages by others who are affected by the decision. He may also seek a court order to enforce his decision, and he may impose a civil fine of up to 10 per cent of the UK turnover of a business if he is satisfied that an infringement has been committed intentionally or negligently.

Appeals[29]

An appeal against a decision or against a fine may be made to the Competition Commission.[30] Third parties who are affected may ask the Director-General to withdraw or vary a decision and may appeal to the Competition Commission if the Director-General rules that he has not been given a sufficient reason to do as they ask.

---

[27] See Annex 3.1 below.
[28] See OFT guide, *The Competition Act 1998: Investigation and Enforcement Procedures*.
[29] See OFT guide, *The Competition Act 1998: Rights of Appeal*.
[30] As described in section D below.

Merger references

Notification

There is no general requirement to notify proposed mergers to the Office of Fair Trading, but companies may seek Confidential Guidance[31] as to whether a merger is likely to be referred to the Competition Commission, and they may seek to speed up their clearance by making informal submissions or by adopting the formal Voluntary Pre-notification Procedure.[32] The final decision whether to make a reference is not made until the merger has been announced and other interested parties have had the opportunity to comment. The Secretary of State may at that stage change his mind in the light of any facts or views that have been brought to his attention. After the submission has been evaluated, the Director-General makes a recommendation to the Secretary of State and the person seeking confidential advice is subsequently informed of the Secretary of State's decision. He may decide:

(a) that the merger appears unlikely to warrant reference; or,
(b) that it is impossible to say whether the merger would warrant reference; or,
(c) that the merger appears to raise competition concerns that would warrant reference, but that such concerns might be remedied by undertakings; or
(d) that the merger appears to warrant reference.

Undertakings

The Director-General may seek undertakings aimed at remedying the adverse effects of a merger as an alternative to recommending a reference. Typically, these may involve the divestment of overlapping activities or promises to refrain from anti-competitive behaviour. If the parties agree, he can then recommend accordingly. The Secretary of State may then either refer the merger, or announce that the merger is to be referred unless satisfactory undertakings are given – or that it is cleared without any undertakings.

---

[31] The information required in a request for confidential guidance is set out in the OFT briefing note *Merger Submissions* (see Appendix 2 for source).
[32] For a merger which has been made public, a decision under this procedure will be made within 20 working days, with a maximum extension of 15 working days (for informal submissions the interval can be up to 45 working days).

References

The procedure by which the Director-General decides whether to recommend the reference of a merger to the Competition Commission is dominated by the need for speed and secrecy. The Office of Fair Trading monitors all mergers and merger proposals and may ask the parties for further information. In some cases, either the Office or the parties may ask for a meeting. A paper prepared from available information, including the parties' submissions, is then despatched to members of the Mergers Panel.[33] In contentious cases, or if a reference is likely, a meeting of the Panel is called at which Office officials present an analysis, departmental officials put forward ministerial or departmental views, and the Director-General makes his decision. The recommendation, which goes to the Secretary of State, is in any case that of the Director-General alone.

D   The Competition Commission

The Competition Commission comprises two bodies with entirely distinct functions:

- the *Appeals Tribunals*, whose function is to decide appeals against decisions of the Director General of Fair Trading;
- the *Reporting Panels* to whom merger and monopoly references may be made, and the *Specialist Panels* who adjudicate disputes between certain public utilities and their regulators.

The Appeals Tribunals

Constitution

Every appeal is decided by an Appeals Tribunal consisting of two members drawn from a panel of members appointed by the Secretary of State and a chairman drawn from a special panel of barristers or otherwise legally qualified persons. The President of the Commission is a judge or senior barrister who is responsible for setting up each tribunal, and who may himself act as a tribunal chairman.

Procedures

Appeals may be made on the grounds of an error of fact or of law, or on the grounds that the Director-General had wrongly exercised his discretion in making a decision or levying a fine. Leave to appeal, or to

---

[33] Consisting of nominees of selected government departments.

amend the grounds of an appeal is at the discretion of the tribunal, but the tribunal's decision must be concerned only with the grounds of the appeal. Appeals may be made either by those against whom the Director-General has made a decision, or by third parties whom the Director-General has judged to have 'sufficient interest' in the decision.[34] Tribunal decisions are based upon hearings at which the substance of the case is re-examined and the parties concerned can make representations. Tribunal decisions need not be unanimous.

Powers

A tribunal may confirm or set aside any part of a decision of the Director-General and may:

(a) remit the matter to the Director-General;
(b) impose, revoke or vary the amount of a penalty;
(c) grant or cancel an individual exemption;
(d) make any direction or decision which is within the powers of the Director-General.

Tribunals cannot undertake independent investigations, however. If substantial new evidence comes to light during an appeal, the case is referred back to the Director-General for investigation.

The reporting and specialist panels

Constitution

The remainder of the Commission took over some of the functions and personnel of the former Monopolies and Mergers Commission and is similarly constituted, with a formal division between members and staff. Members are appointed by the Secretary of State and are responsible for the contents of the reports made to him. The staff are appointed by the Commission and their functions are to collect and analyse information, to prepare drafts of the Commission's reports and to give advice.

Members are appointed for their ability and experience, and not as representatives of particular interests. (In 1998 the reporting panel members numbered 40 from a wide range of professions[35] and a further 13 members served on specialist panels concerned with newspaper, water, electricity and telecommunications references.) Members are appointed for renewable five-year terms. The Chairman of the Commission is

---

[34] And third parties may appeal against his decision.
[35] Eight company directors, seven accountants, five lawyers, three economists, three trade union officials and three former civil servants.

appointed by the Secretary of State from among the reporting panel members, the remainder of whom are engaged on a part-time basis. The staff is headed by the Commission Secretary (who is appointed by the Secretary of State) and includes accountants, economists and legal advisers.

Reporting Panel procedures

The procedures adopted for mergers inquiries are substantially the same as those used by the former Monopolies and Mergers Commission. Broadly similar procedures are likely to be adopted for any monopoly or public sector inquiries that arise.

Preliminaries

(a)   A Group of not less than three members, appointed by the Chairman, conducts an inquiry chaired (usually) by himself or one of the Deputy Chairmen. A team of officials is brought together to support the Group throughout the inquiry, including a Team Manager, a Reference Secretary and selected staff from the specialist divisions.

(b)   The Reference Secretary circulates a background paper summarising available information, together with a draft work programme and timetable for the main stages of the inquiry. This has to be strictly tailored to the time-limit stipulated in the reference.

Fact-finding

(c)   It is first necessary to establish that a statutory merger situation[36] exists. Written submissions are invited from parties concerned and from other interested parties. The main parties are then asked to make written submissions of their case for when it is contested.

(d)   The staff then present summaries of the information which they have obtained to the Group, drawing attention to issues which the Group might consider to be relevant to their inquiry.

Hearings

(e)   The Commission may offer interested parties the opportunity to attend – or to raise the issues which are relevant to the inquiry. Hearings take place in private, normally with each party appearing separately. Statements by the parties are followed by questions from members of the Group. The procedure adopted is intended to be investigatory not adversarial, but parties may be legally represented if they so wish. A verbatim record of the proceedings is made, and sent to each party for checking.

---

[36] See section D in Chapter 2 above.

(f) After further discussions, the staff prepare and obtain the Group's approval for the issue of an *Issues Letter* to the principal parties. The Group will not at this stage have reached any conclusion concerning the public interest, and the purpose is to warn those who are to attend the main hearing of the issues about which the Group will wish to ask questions. In recent years, issues letters have been published to inform other parties who may wish to make submissions.

(g) At the main hearing, the procedure is as described in (e) above, but the public interest letter, or the list of issues, is used as the agenda. The main purpose is to give those attending an opportunity to respond to any points which might be interpreted as criticisms of their behaviour or proposals. The occasion may also be taken to discuss possible remedies for any matters that might be found to be against the public interest.[37] If necessary, there may be a further hearing to discuss remedies.

Reporting

(h) Work is in the meantime in hand on drafts of the factual portion of the Group's report. The Reference Secretary draws together contributions from other members of the team, and drafts are progressively 'put back' to those who provided the information for comments on factual accuracy, and any representations concerning confidentiality. At appropriate stages, the drafts are also put to the Group for comment or approval. After the conclusion of the hearings, the Group meet to discuss proposed conclusions and recommendations, and to consider drafts of the concluding sections of their report. There are no consultations with outsiders concerning the Group's public-interest conclusions.

(i) There is finally a 'settle and sign' meeting of the Group at which final amendments are made and each member signs a copy of the report, and at which those who disagree with the majority conclusion may table statements of their dissent for incorporation in the report.

E   The Secretary of State

The Secretary of State for Trade and Industry is the cabinet minister responsible for the formulation of British competition policy, and he has limited powers over its execution. He appoints the Director-General

[37] See page 30.

of Fair Trading and the members of the Competition Commission and may issue general rules and directions concerning the conduct of their duties. Under certain conditions, he may alter the list of practices excluded from the prohibition of Chapter I of the Competition Act. He may act in accordance with recommendations from the Director-General of Fair Trading concerning the authorisation of block exemptions and concerning the reference of mergers to the Competition Commission, but he is not bound to do so. He may call upon the Director-General to seek undertakings in lieu of merger references, and he may prohibit a merger or stipulate conditions under which it is permitted, but only when the Commission has ruled that the merger would be against the public interest.[38] Reasons must be given for some of these actions and it is customary to give reasons for most of them.

F The courts

The criminal courts have no jurisdiction under British competition law except in respect of the offences of deliberately providing false or misleading information to the competition authorities and of obstructing the Director-General's rights of access to information. It is not an offence to defy an order by the Director-General but to do so is to provide grounds for an action for damages. Breach of a court order obtained to enforce his decision can be punished as contempt of court.

Contracts that infringe Chapter 1 of the Competition Act or Article 81 of the Treaty of Amsterdam are void and cannot be enforced in the courts. Such infringements can be the subject of actions for damages in the civil courts. An allegation of infringement by the plaintiff has been used as a defence against an action for breach of contract.[39] Actions for damages can also be taken against companies that breach the prohibitions of Chapter 2 or Article 82.[40] Appeals can be made to the Court of Appeal against the rulings of the Competition Commission on matters of law or penalties. The civil courts must take account of statements made by the European Commission, but cannot issue exemptions from the prohibitions of restrictive agreements caught by Article 81(1).[41] British courts may seek a ruling on interpretation of Community law

[38] See the DTI guide, Appendix 2.
[39] *British Leyland v Wyatt 1979.*
[40] *Garden Cottage 1983.*
[41] See Notice on Cooperation between National Courts and the Commission in Applying Articles 85 and 86 of the Treaty OJ C93/6 1993.

from the European Court, and the Court of Appeal can be required to do so.[42]

The civil courts can also exercise a degree of supervision over the regulatory authorities themselves. In common with the actions of other regulatory authorities, the competition policy decisions of the Secretary of State, the Director-General of Fair Trading and the Competition Commission may be challenged in the High Court under a procedure which is termed judicial review. The three accepted grounds for judicial review (illegality, irrationality and procedural irregularity) have been explained in the following terms:

> proceedings for judicial review are not concerned with the correctness of the decision . . . but with the means by which the decision was reached. It is no part of the court's function in such proceedings to make a new decision . . . but to consider the legitimacy of the process by which the decision was reached, the relevance or validity of the considerations of which account was taken, and the admissibility or probative value of the evidence upon which the decision was based.[43]

Judicial review could in principle provide a remedy for the wrongful conduct of a mergers case, but so far, all attempts to do so have failed.

G   International relations

Relations between national competition authorities are governed by the non-binding legal principle of the comity of nations. That principle has been described as 'aiming at balancing the exercise of extraterritorial jurisdiction with a readiness on behalf of the country enforcing its competition laws to take into account the important interests of another country'.[44] The procedures adopted follow proposals by the OECD.[45] The present agreement on the matter between the European Union and the United States follows a previous (1991) agreement in extending the concept to that of positive comity.[46] The agreement applies where

---

[42]   As provided by Article 177 of the Treaty.
[43]   *ICI 1986*.
[44]   Kiriazis 1998.
[45]   Revised Recommendation of the Council Concerning Cooperation between Member States on Anticompetitive Practices Affecting International Trade, OECD C(95) 130/FINAL 27/28 July 1995.
[46]   Agreement between the European Communities and the Government of the United States of America regarding the application of positive comity principles in the enforcement of their competition laws OJ L 173 June 1998.

(a)   anticompetitive activities are occurring in . . . the territory of one of the Parties and are adversely affecting the interests of the other Party; and,

(b)   the activities in question are impermissible under the competition laws of the Party in the territory of which the activities are occurring.

The agreement specifies the circumstances under which a party will be presumed to suspend its own enforcement activities and outlines procedures for the exchange of information – subject, however, to national confidentiality undertakings. Cooperation was particularly important in obtaining undertakings from Boeing about its merger with MDD[47] and although the present agreement provides more limited coverage of merger cases, there has been continuing cooperation.[48]

Annex 3.1:   Confidentiality

Information cannot be withheld from the regulatory authorities on the grounds that its disclosure would be incriminating. However, privileged information, such as is exchanged between a lawyer and his client, need not be disclosed and there are certain safeguards concerning its subsequent disclosure.

European Community Practice

Commission and member states may not disclose information of the kind covered by the obligation of professional secrecy.[49] Where the Commission considers disclosure to be necessary to its investigation, it must give advance warning to the owner, who may then apply to the European Court to prevent it. The Commission must publish the names of the parties and the main content of every decision, but in doing so, it is required to 'have regard to the legitimate interest of undertakings in the protection of their business secrets'.[50] The prohibition must be presumed not to apply to the disclosure of information to the Competent Authorities of member states nor to members of the Advisory Committee on Restrictive Practices and Monopolies, both of whom are entitled to be informed.[51] The information obtained may only be used for the purpose of the relevant request or investigation.[52] Applicants are

[47]   see Schaub 1998.
[48]   For example, in the Dresser/Haliburton case, IP/98/643.
[49]   Regulation 17 Art. 20.
[50]   Ibid., Art. 21.
[51]   Ibid., Art. 11.
[52]   Ibid., Art. 20.

asked to put confidential information in a separate annex and to give reasons why it should not be published.

Commission practice concerning the disclosure of information to the United States authorities is governed by the 1991 EC/US agreement.[53]

United Kingdom practice

Information obtained under UK competition law may not be disclosed without the permission of the business concerned, except in pursuance of a Community obligation or for the purpose of criminal proceedings, of a Community obligation or of facilitating the performance of the competition authorities.[54] The prohibition is not absolute because it expressly does not limit the content of the reports of the Competition Commission, and the Competition Act gives limited powers of disclosure to the Secretary of State.

The Office of Fair Trading has indicated that people making complaints alleging a breach of a prohibition should make it clear at the earliest opportunity if they consider that they need to have their identity concealed.

It has been the invariable practice of the former Monopolies and Mergers Commission to invite the providers of information to indicate any parts of it that they wish not to be disclosed. This is done during the drafting of their reports, as a part of the putting-back[55] procedures. In making its reports, the Commission has a statutory duty[56] to have regard to the need for excluding, so far as that is practicable, matters the publication of which might in its opinion seriously and prejudicially affect the interests of those concerned. There is, however, the proviso 'unless in the opinion of the Commission...the inclusion of that matter...is necessary for the purposes of the report'. The Secretary of State may then arrange for the excision from the published report of any passages whose publication would in his opinion be against the public interest. Representations from firms on such matters are treated sympathetically, and many of the published reports exhibit blank spaces where such excisions have been made.

---

[53] Statement on Confidentiality of Information 10/4/95.
[54] As required by s133 of the Fair Trading Act 1973 and s55 of the Competition Act 1998.
[55] See section D in Chapter 3 above.
[56] Under s82(3) of the Fair Trading Act 1973.

Part II

The Regulation of Business Practices

4
The Assessment of Market Power

A   Introduction

The importance of market power

Market power is the crucial concept of competition policy because it determines its possessor's ability to impose an economic loss[1] on the community. It is the basis on which regulatory jurisdiction is defined and it has a strong influence upon regulatory practice.

A firm that has less than an arbitrary minimum of market power is deemed to be outside the scope of competition policy[2]. Market share[3] is used as a surrogate for market power for that purpose, among others. The extent of the firm's influence upon prices determines the appropriate extent of market to be included, as regards geographical extent and as regards product range. The alternatives which are likely to be available to customers limit the scope of the relevant market in both of those respects.

Some such alternatives are taken into account in determining jurisdiction, while others are taken into account only after the firm's conduct comes under investigation.

The treatment of a firm which falls within the scope of the legislation is strongly influenced by the magnitude of its market power. The possession

---

[1] By departures from *optimum resource allocation* as discussed in section A of Chapter 1.

[2] For instance, most *agreements* (except price fixing or market-sharing) are exempt unless the market shares involved exceed 25 per cent; the possession of a *dominant position* is likely to be assumed when a firm's market share reaches 40–45 per cent, and cannot be ruled out for shares as low as 20 per cent; and a *merger situation* requires either a combined market share of at least 25 per cent or the acquisition of assets above a stipulated limit.

[3] Normally measured in terms of sales value.

of market power is not prohibited, but the regulators seek to limit its acquisition by mergers, inter-company agreements, and anti-competitive behaviour; and sometimes to limit its exercise. In estimating the degree of a company's market power for that purpose, account is taken of the extent to which the exercise of market power is likely to be limited by the prospects that competitors will enter the market, and by the countervailing market power of buyers.

The content of this chapter is thus essential to the understanding of much of what follows. It deals first, in section B, with the question of market definition; and then, in section C, with the broader question of market power; and in sections D and E with the effects of entry prospects and buying power.

B   Market definition

The guidelines

Previous editions of this book attempted to explain the market definition used by each of the competition authorities by reference to their treatment of it in individual cases. Some uncertainties and inconsistencies were evident. In 1997, however, – following the example of the US Department of Justice – both the UK and the EU authorities issued similar guidelines[4] of which the following is a summary.

Basic principles

A market is defined for competition policy purposes in terms of a product range and a geographical sales area. These are defined by EU legislation[5] in the following terms:

> A relevant product market comprises all those products and/or services which are regarded as interchangeable or substitutable by the consumer, by reason of the products' characteristics, their prices and their intended use.
>
> A relevant geographic market comprises the area in which the undertakings concerned are involved in the supply and demand of products or services, in which the conditions of competition are sufficiently homogeneous and which can be distinguished from neighbouring areas because the conditions of competition are appreciably different in those areas.

---

[4] See Appendix 1 at the end of the book.
[5] Commission Notice on the relevant market OJ C372 9/12/97.

The problem is how to define those markets in a way that is relevant to the possession of market power. Too narrow a definition would exclude substitutes which limit market power, so that the possession of a particular market share would give an exaggerated impression of market power. (The true market power represented by a 100 per cent share in the market for apples, for example, would be limited by the willingness of customers to accept other forms of fresh fruit as substitutes.) Too broad a definition would include products which have little influence on the market for the supplier's product so that a given market share would tend to understate the supplier's market power. (The hypothetical apple monopolist might have less than one per cent of the market for all food, but his true market power would be higher than that figure would suggest.) The authorities' solution has been the qualified[6] adoption of the definition by the United States Department of Justice of an antitrust market:

> a product or group of products and a geographical area in which it is sold, such that a hypothetical profit-maximising firm ... that was the only present and future seller of those products in that area would impose a small but significant and nontransitory increase in price above prevailing or likely future levels.[7]

The procedure implied by this definition starts with the actual product – or geographical – market supplied by the firm, and considers the likely consumer reaction to a small (e.g. 5 per cent) price increase. If purchasers then switch to an alternative product – or location – the market is redefined to include that product – or location. The hypothetical price increase is then applied to the redefined market, and the process is continued until no further switching occurs.

The following paragraphs first describe the application of these principles to product markets and to geographical markets, and then turn to the more complex issue of *supply-side substitution*.

Product market definition

The OFT and European Commission guides describe how they apply the above procedure to product markets, noting that the information involved varies from case to case. The existence of separate markets

---

[6] The qualification is that the increases are hypothesised to be above the *competitive price,* not the *prevailing price* in cases where the price has already been raised above the competitive level.
[7] The US DoJ's 1992 Merger Guidelines.

can in some cases be inferred from the fact that there are few purchasers who buy in both markets; but in some cases, extensive enquiries and analysis are necessary to settle the matter.[8] The concept of *cross-price elasticity* (the effect on sales of product Y of a price increase of product X) is sometimes employed, and an OFT research paper (NERA 1992) describes how it can be estimated. Among practical complications is the possibility of the exercise of market power by price discrimination against *captive customers* who, for some reason (such as lack of mobility), are unable to switch to substitutes. The major complication, however, is the existence of *chains of substitution*. The example cited by the OFT places the Volkswagen Polo in the same market as the Mercedes, despite the probable absence of direct substitution between them.[9]

Among the many concrete examples of decisions[10] relating to product-market definition that may be referred to, some of those which appear to be in line with current practice are:

- the UK market for cola drinks is distinct from the market for other soft drinks, because consumers say that they would not switch in response to a small price increase (*Coca Cola/Amalgamated Beverages 1997*);
- there are distinct markets for matches and cigarette-lighters with little correlation despite their functional interchangeability; (*Swedish Match/KAV 1997*);
- the market for tyres for trucks and buses is different from that for cars (*Michelin 1983*);
- pneumatic power-tools are close substitutes for electric power-tools (*Atlas Copco/Desoutter 1990**);
- the market for travellers' cheques is distinct from that for credit cards (*Thomas Cook/ISL 1995**);
- motorway restaurants are a separate market (*Accor/Wagons Lits 1992*, the contrary finding in *Happy Eater/Little Chef 1987** being an aberration);
- there are three distinct markets for commuter aircraft with different seating capacities, as established by economic analysis of demand patterns (*Aerospatiale/Alenia/de Havilland 1991*);

[8] As in *ITS/Signode/Titan 1998* described below.
[9] Assuming that a price increase for the Polo would lead buyers to switch to (e.g.) the Ford Escort, that category of car would have to be included, and so on through (e.g.) the Mondeo to the top of the range.
[10] Decisions marked * were made by the former MMC and were not intended to set precedents.

- the market for packaging machines for cartons is distinct from that for packaging machines for glass and plastics because customer surveys had shown there to be a low cross-elasticity of demand between them (*TetraPak/Alpha Laval 1991*);
- vitamins supplied for medicinal use compete in a different market because consumption patterns are substantially different from those for the same vitamins supplied for industrial use (*Hoffman-La Roche 1979*);
- the appearance of dominance in the market for steel strapping was found to be misleading when enquiries among customers revealed that plastic strapping was a close substitute (*ITS/Signode/ Titan 1998*).

The OFT guide notes that market definitions may vary with changes in market conditions and according to the practice under consideration.

Geographical markets

The OFT guide notes that the existence of a *chain of substitution* could in principle lead to an indefinite extension of a geographical market unless there were a break in the chain. In relation to commercial transactions, the European Commission guide refers to the progressive integration of the internal market, and it has sometimes been prepared to anticipate the removal of trade-barriers between member states. The extent of the integration of retail markets, however, is normally limited by breaks in the chain, for example in rural areas or at the coast.

Among the factors which have been taken into account in some of the cases[11] that illustrate the practice of defining geographical markets have been:

- customers' reluctance to travel too far to buy food (*Promodes/BRMC 1992*), to visit the pub (*Scottish & Newcastle/Matthew Brown 1985**) or to place a bet (*Ladbrook/Coral 1998*);[12]
- the local nature of the services provided (e.g. in the multitude of bus cases);
- high transport costs in relation to selling costs (in *Ready Mixed Concrete 1981** and – for bricks – in *Tarmac/Steetley 1992** but this

---

[11] Decisions marked * were made by the former MMC and were not intended to set precedents.
[12] Beyond a 440-metre radius, but *GrandMet/William Hill 1989* adopted a nationwide market.

consideration was outweighed by chain of substitution considerations in *Pilkington/SIV 1993*);
- geographical differences of consumer preferences (for bottled water in *Nestlé/Perrier 1992* and for ice-cream in *Unilever/Ortiz 1994*);
- the availability of overseas supplies (of sugar in *Berisford/British Sugar 1981** and – even in the absence of actual import penetration – as a reason for not referring a merger which created a 94 per cent share of the UK market for automotive bearings, as reported in *The Guardian* of 12 May 1988);
- external tariffs (which, at 7 per cent, confined to the EU what might otherwise have been a world market in *Solvay/Laporte 1992*);
- trade barriers within the EU (which, for gas-pipes, restricted to Germany an otherwise community-wide market in *Mannesmann/Hoesch 1992*, but were not considered a restriction because of their projected expiry for rubber car-parts in *BTR/Pirelli 1992*);
- the purchasing practices of commercial buyers (which created world markets for aircraft in *Aerospatiale/Alenia/de Havilland 1991* and for commercial chemicals in *Merck/Alginates 1979**);
- the world market for internet services and the consequent need for joint action with other competition authorities (*Worldcom/MCI 1998*).

Supply-side substitution

A firm's market power can be limited by the prospect that its exercise could attract the entry of new competitors into the market for its products. There are two ways of looking at this. One is to regard the prospects of such an entry as one of the factors which may offset the market power consequence of the possession of a high market-share. The other is to regard it as a determining factor in defining the relevant market. Under the latter approach, the possibility of *supply-side substitution* can lead to the extension of the relevant market to include other products whose production capacity can be switched to the supply of the product in question. An example is the supply of paper for use in publishing. Paper is produced in various grades, depending on the coating used. Users do not regard the different grades as substitutes, but market power over any particular grade is limited by the fact that manufacturers can easily switch production from one grade to another.

Although the choice between these alternative approaches should not in principle affect the outcome, it can make a great deal of difference to the businesses affected. A procedure which relieves them of the burden of an investigation is obviously preferable to one which exonerates them as a result of an investigation. The avoidance of unnecessary work for the competition authorities could also be argued in its favour. The OFT guide notes that

> Defining markets on the supply-side can allow us to determine at an early stage that a firm does not have market power, avoiding the need for further analysis.

The otherwise academic question of when supply-side substitution should affect the determination of the relevant market is thus of considerable practical concern.

The limits on its use by the European Commission are noted in their guide in the following terms:

> When supply side substitutability would imply the need to adjust significantly existing tangible and intangible assets, additional investments, strategic decisions or time delays, it will not be considered at the stage of market definition.
>
> Examples where supply side substitution did not lead the Commission to enlarge the market are offered in the area of consumer products, in particular for branded beverages. Although bottling plants may in principle bottle different beverages, there are costs and lead times involved (in terms of advertising, product testing and distribution) before the products can actually be sold. In these cases, the effects of supply side substitutability and other forms of potential competition would then be examined at a later stage.

The OFT guide is more specific:

> If substitution took longer than one year these firms would not normally be included in the market.... Even if substitution is technically possible, there may be barriers. For example, cat and dog foods are produced using similar technology, and substitution is technically feasible. However, a firm switching between them might need to spend time establishing a brand in a new product area, so substitution could not occur in the short term.... The Office will therefore include supply-side substitutes within the market definition when it is clear that substitution would take place quickly. If there is any serious doubt on this point, they will not be included....

There are few concrete examples of the practical application of supply-side substitution to market definition that can reliably be used as a guide to future practice. The concept does not figure in the reports of the former Monopolies and Mergers Commission, and there have been inconsistencies in its past use by the European Commission.[13] The OFT guide refers to *Continental Can 1973* (in which the European Court overturned a Commission decision because of its failure to define the market correctly) and *Torras/Sarrio 1992*.

C   Market power

The importance of market power

Market power gives its possessor a degree of choice concerning the prices he may charge and the consequent levels of sales which he may expect.[14] It is the crucial concept of competition theory because it is a measure of the economic loss which can be imposed upon the rest of the community by distorting consumer choice away from the cost-related basis which rules under pure competition. There is no presumption in UK or EU competition policy that market power is harmful in itself, but measures of market power are widely used as indicators of the magnitude of possible losses of allocative efficiency.[15] They can be of decisive importance in cases in which such losses have to be weighed against possible gains in productive efficiency. Market power is not solely a characteristic of its possessor, but depends also upon the reactions of his customers. Customers may react in a variety of ways. If they respond to an increase in the price of one product by switching their purchases to a close substitute, their behaviour thereby limits both the exercise of market power to increase the price of that product, and the amount of economic damage that it can do. If, on the other hand, they respond by switching some of their purchases to an entirely different category of product, resources are misallocated to a greater extent and there may be a substantial loss of economic welfare.[16] A price increase which leads to the substitution of one type of thermal insulation for another is clearly of less significance than one which leads to a switch of expenditure into energy consumption. If, however, customers are relatively insensitive to price changes, a price increase may result mainly in a transfer of resources to the producer, with a minimal distortion of expenditure patterns and little loss of total welfare. An increase in bread prices, for example, may have little effect on bread consumption.

---

[13] According to Neven, Nuttall and Seabright 1993.
[14] As explained further in section B of Chapter 1 above.
[15] Defined in section B of Chapter 1 above.
[16] Meaning the extent to which people feel themselves to be well-off.

A supplier's market power may also be reduced or eliminated if his customers enjoy market power as buyers. The extent of a supplier's market power depends also upon the reactions of his rivals. If the originator of a price increase is looked upon as a price leader, other suppliers may match his increase. Otherwise he will lose sales to them to the extent that their products are seen as substitutes for his. He may also face the danger that his price increase may prompt the entry of new producers into the market.

Dominance

The term *dominant position* which appears in Chapter II of the Competition Act, Article 82 of the Treaty of Amsterdam[17] and in the EU merger regulation has been defined in the following terms:

> a position of economic strength enjoyed by an undertaking which enables it to hinder the maintenance of effective competition in the relevant market by allowing it to behave to an appreciable extent independently of its competitors and customers.[18]

EU law does not stipulate a market share criterion for dominance, but the Commission has stated[19] that

> A dominant position can generally be said to exist once a market share to the order of 40 per cent to 45 per cent has been reached, although this share does not in itself automatically give control of the market, if there are large gaps between the position of the firm concerned and those of its closest competitors and also other factors ... as regards competition. ...

In practice the absence of a market share above 20 per cent has been taken as adequate evidence of the absence of dominance, but higher market shares need not indicate its presence, because of the other factors referred to. The unquantifiable nature of those other factors means that there can be no objective definition of dominance, and that their treatment of past cases often provides the only guide to the authorities' future judgements on the matter. Among the factors other than market share which are taken into account the most important are the prospect of the entry of a competitor, and the countervailing power of buyers.

---

[17] Formerly Article 86 of the Rome Treaty.
[18] *Michelin v Commission 1983.*
[19] Competition Report 10, 1980, point 150.

Joint dominance

Article 82 of the Treaty of Amsterdam and Chapter II of the Competition Act refer to conduct on the part of *one or more* undertakings, i.e. to a position of *joint dominance*. The OFT has defined joint dominance as occurring when undertakings are linked in such a way that they adopt the same conduct in the market. The European Court of First Instance has noted that

> there is nothing in principle to prevent two or more independent economic entities from being, in a specific market, united by such economic links that, by virtue of that fact they hold a dominant position vis-à-vis the other operator in the same market[20]

The network effect

An additional consideration relating to communications systems is that the value of a network to its user increases non-linearly with its size – from a negligible value when few contacts can be made, to great value when – like the postal system – it enables most people to be reached. This *network effect* can lead to product *lock-in*[21] and can confer greater market power on a large operator than its market share would suggest. It was decisive in forcing the divestment of overlapping internet activities as a condition for clearance of a telecoms merger (*Worldcom/MCI 1998*).

D   Entry prospects

Entry strategies

A potential entrant to a market in which the dominant firm has set prices at above the competitive level must be assumed to take account of the prospect that his entry will lead to a reduction in those prices. Accordingly, he must choose between two strategies:

(a) to make a temporary incursion into the market in order to take advantage of the period during which prices remain high, and to withdraw before they fall to a level at which it is no longer profitable for him to compete; or,

(b) to plan for a sustained entry, and to seek a position in which he can at least match the unit costs and quality of the dominant firm, and can thus continue to compete even after prices have been driven down to their competitive level; ...

---

[20] *Italian Flat Glass* Cases T-68/69 &c 5 CMLR 302.
[21] In which the costs of change prevent purchasers from switching.

These are termed, respectively, *uncommitted entry* and *committed entry*. If there is a plausible threat of either strategy being adopted, it may be assumed to deter the dominant firm from overcharging. But an established firm may be assumed to enjoy some advantages over a newcomer, and unless the dominant firm is evidently inefficient, the potential entrant may face considerable risks. Those risks can, however, be eliminated if the initial investment which is required for entry can later be recovered without loss. The market is then termed contestable[22] and uncommitted entry is a commercially attractive strategy. Perfect contestability is rarely approached, however, and a threat of uncommitted entry is unlikely to be a plausible influence on market power. Nevertheless, the risks incurred, in what is intended to be committed entry, are the smaller, the lower are the net costs of entry and of exit.

Decisions[23] that entry prospects completely offset the possession of high market shares have included:

- a merger between the two largest manufacturers of synthetic fibres in Europe, giving them a combined market share of 65 per cent (*Courtaulds/SNIA 1991*);
- the takeover by the UK's largest tour operator of its third largest tour operator (*Thomson/Horizon 1989**);
- a merger which raised Parker's share of the low-priced fountain-pen market from 74 per cent to 80 per cent and gave it 72 per cent of the fountain-pen market as a whole (*Gillette/Parker Pen 1993**);
- a merger between operators of local bus services giving a combined market share of 65 per cent (*SB Holdings/Kelvin Central Buses 1995**);
- a merger which gave two airlines a 50 per cent market share (*Air France/Sabena 1992*);
- a shipping merger yielding a 72 per cent market share (*Trafalgar House/P&O 1984**).

Speed of entry

The effect of entry prospects upon market power depends upon the speed with which entry could be expected. Long-term entry prospects have generally been assumed to have a negligible effects. The possibility of rapid entry has, on the other hand, been considered decisive and has

---

[22] The concept of contestability is discussed in section B of Chapter 1 above (p. 10).
[23] Decisions marked * were made by the former MMC and were not intended to set precedents.

usually been taken into account in defining the relevant market.[24] The few decisions which offer specific guidance include:

- the prospect of entry into the commuter aircraft market, with a lag of six years, did not offset other evidence of dominance (*Aerospatiale/Alenia/de Havilland 1991*);
- the prospect of new entry into the tyre market could not be taken into account because of the time necessary to build or modify a factory for the purpose (*Michelin 1983*);
- the prospect of new entry into the car-parts market was, however, taken into account because the time-lag would be only two years (*Lucas/Eaton 1991*);
- a high market share in the supply of cans for preserving food did not confer dominance because manufacturers of other types of can could readily adapt their equipment in order to compete in its markets (*Continental Can 1973*);
- a merger which led to a combined market share of over 80 per cent of the Spanish market for telecommunications equipment was approved because the only customer was prepared to buy from abroad (*Alcatel/Telettra 1991*).

Entry barriers

The barriers which the authorities have taken into account in assessing entry prospects have included capital requirements, product differentiation, network effects, regulatory barriers, access to essential facilities, predatory pricing and exclusive dealing.[25] Decisions[26] which throw some light upon the likely treatment of such factors include the categorisation as effective barriers to entry of:

- the investment required for large-scale salt production (which precluded the possibility of a competitor challenging the high prices charged by ICI) (*White Salt 1986**);
- the difficulty of obtaining an adequate rate of return on investment (on an entry cost of between £360 thousand and £1 million in a market for roofing systems of about £12 million a year) (*MiTek/Gang Nail 1988*);

[24] See *supply-side substitution* in section B of Chapter 2 above (p. 66).
[25] The barriers created by predatory behaviour are dealt with in section C of Chapter 6 below and those created by exclusive dealing and licensing and access to essential facilities are dealt with in Chapter 7.
[26] Decisions marked * were made by the former MMC and were not intended to set precedents.

- the promotional expenditure required to break into mail-order retailing (*GUS/Empire 1983**);
- the possession of substantial technological leads over potential entrants ((*United Brands 1978, Hoffman-La Roche 1979* and *Michelin 1983*);
- brand images (of 'Chiquita' for bananas, 'Calor Gas' for bottled butane and 'Durex' for contraceptives) (*United Brands 1978, Liquefied Petroleum Gas 1981** and *Contraceptive Sheaths 1982**);
- a proven track record in connection with health and safety on the part of a supplier of food packaging equipment (*TetraPak/Alpha Laval 1991*);
- overcapacity in a market for bulk chemicals (*Du Pont/ICI 1992*);
- network effects upon internet services (*Worldcom/MCI 1998*).
- regulatory barriers concerning telecommunications equipment, motorway restaurants and the licensing of betting shops (*Alcatel/ Telettra 1991, Accor/Wagons-Lits 1992* and *Grand Metropolitan/William Hill 1989**) and also in the case of *Contact Lens Solutions 1993**.

E   The countervailing power of buyers

Dominance is unlikely to be ascribed to suppliers to powerful buyers – as is illustrated by the following decisions:

- that a merger which eliminated all competition from the safety-glass industry was not against the public interest because of the bargaining power of the industry's main suppliers (*Flat Glass 1968*, p 293*);
- that a merger of suppliers of personalised cheques which gave them a combined market share was not against the public interest because of the bargaining power of the banks who were their only customers (*Norton Opax/McCorquodale 1986**);
- that the high levels of concentration in food manufacturing were not a matter of concern in view of the bargaining power of the large supermarket chains (*Discounts to Retailers 1981**);
- that a merger between suppliers of communications equipment yielding a combined market share of 83 per cent was acceptable in view of the buying power of national purchasing agencies (*Alcatel/ Telettra 1991*);
- that a merger between two of the six largest accounting firms was acceptable because the customary use of long-term contracts and of competitive tendering by their clients would lead to the exclusion of an unsatisfactory incumbent (*Price Waterhouse/Coopers & Lybrand 1998*);

- that a merger which created the largest integrated paper and board group in the world was acceptable mainly because of the countervailing power of the large publishing groups (*Enso/Stora 1998*).

F   Conclusion: the treatment of market power

It is evident that no precise definition of market power is feasible, and that some discretionary action by the authorities is therefore unavoidable. Some uncertainties are thereby introduced concerning their treatment of business behaviour.

Those uncertainties are being reduced to some extent by analytical developments which are embodied in their reports and by their published guidelines. The variety of business experience and innovation is so great, however, that regulatory practice is constantly evolving. The foregoing analysis has summarised the present intellectual background and indicated the cases which provide a more detailed guide to regulatory practice in particular circumstances. In most respects, the treatment of market power has reached a stage of maturity at which little in the way of further development is to be expected – except, possibly, in the evaluation of network effects. If there is any doubt about a company's compliance, it would be prudent, nevertheless, to scan recent bulletins for regulatory developments.

5
The Control of Mergers and Joint Ventures

A Introduction

Policy presumptions

The operation of merger policy depends less upon the enabling legislation and its investigatory procedures than upon the presumption which is adopted concerning the general effect of mergers on the public interest. A balance has to be struck between expected losses of allocative efficiency resulting from the reduction of competition and expected gains in productive efficiency;[1] and different authorities may adopt different presumptions in that respect. In an early case,[2] the European Court of Justice ruled that an increase in the market share of a dominant undertaking can on its own constitute a breach of the Treaty of Rome. European Union merger regulation is not now confined to dominant undertakings, but it does not seek to prevent mergers unless they impede effective competition. The regulation stipulates that account is to be taken of technical and economic progress which is to the consumers' advantage, but only if no obstacle to competition is created. In practice, however, efficiency gains are often balanced against losses of competition. The Commission is, moreover, required[3] to place its appraisal within the general framework of the fundamental objectives of Article 2 of the Treaty of Rome, which included the following :

---

[1] See page 5.
[2] *Continental Can 1973.*
[3] Rehearsal 13 to Regulation 4064/89 confirmed by the Court of First Instance in *Perrier Union 1992.*

to promote ... a harmonious and balanced development of economic activities, sustainable and non-inflationary growth respecting the environment, a high degree of convergence of economic employment, a high level of employment and of social protection, the raising of the standard of living and quality of life, and economic and social cohesion among member states.

The promotion of competition is only one of the objectives to be sought under British merger legislation. The legislation, also, requires the promotion of technical progress to be sought through competition. But in considering where the public interest lies, those objectives have to be balanced against a number of others. British practice is to permit a merger to proceed, even if it leads to a substantial increase in market power, unless there is convincing evidence that it will be against the public interest. The attitude of the former Monopolies and Mergers Commission in that respect was illustrated by statements made in two of their reports. Concerning the proposed merger of Britain's largest sugar merchant with its largest sugar producer, one group commented that:

> The question we have to consider is not merely whether there is a possibility that the merger will operate against the public interest. If only a possibility were required, hardly any merger could be allowed to proceed, for it is very rarely that such a possibility can be quite excluded. The question is whether the merger will operate against the public interest. To put the matter colloquially, the required conclusion is not, 'This may happen' but 'We expect that this will happen'.
> *(Berisford/British Sugar 1981*, par 9.40)

In that case, the Commission concluded that 'we find no respects in which the merger may be expected to produce clear benefits in relation to the public interest' but the merger was allowed to proceed. Another investigating group observed that:

> we discern no material advantages to the public interest arising from the proposed merger; but the question before us is whether the merger may be expected to operate against the public interest, and in our view there are not sufficient grounds for such an expectation.
> *(Scottish & Newcastle/Matthew Brown 1985*, par 7.13)

A 1978 policy review noted that existing policy was biased in favour of mergers, and recommended a move to a more neutral position, but its recommendation was rejected.[4] Government policy at that time was stated in a 1988 White Paper in the following terms:

> The Government believe that there are considerable benefits from allowing freedom for change in corporate ownership and control through mergers and acquisitions. Generally, the market will be a better arbiter than Government of the prospects for the proposed transactions, and will ensure better use of assets, for the benefit of their owners and the economy as a whole. Government should intervene only where the interests of the decision-makers in the market are likely to run counter to the public interest. The classic example of this is where a merger threatens to give the newly-formed enterprise a position of market power which it will be able to exploit at the expense of its customers.[5]

The benefits from mergers which are referred to in that policy statement were expected to arise from the theory of the *market for corporate control*. According to that theory, management teams compete for the right to control corporate assets, and management efficiency is ensured by a natural selection mechanism in which takeovers, or the threat of takeovers, ensure the survival of the fittest. Poor management performance leads to a weak share price, encouraging a corporate raider to seize the opportunity to make capital gains by installing a better management team and reaping the benefit in the form of the resulting increase in the share price (Meade, 1968). The proposition that the threat of a takeover is an effective spur to managerial efficiency has received some empirical support from a study of UK mergers (Holl and Pickering, 1986). However, that study and many others[6] also indicate that mergers do not, on average, lead to efficiency gains.

A further review of UK mergers policy was initiated in 1998, the results of which were not available when this book went to press.

The prospects of abuse

Different presumptions may also be adopted as to whether market power is likely to be abused. The Monopolies and Mergers Commission have often presumed that it will not. A merger which virtually eliminated

---

[4] DTI 1978.
[5] Cm 279, quoted in full in DTI 1988, Annex C.
[6] See DTI 1988, Annex E, and Chiplin and Wright 1987, Chapter 7, for summaries of such studies.

competition in the supply of mineral-insulated cable, and from which no great economic benefits were expected, was not opposed by the Commission because of assurances provided by the acquiring company (*BICC/Pyrotenax 1967*), and in commenting upon an acquisition which gave Pilkington control of the British safety-glass industry, the group concerned said that:

> we do not think that Pilkington is to be criticised for seeking to control the safety glass industry in this country.... We are satisfied that Pilkington is conscious of its responsibility as a monopolist, to the public interest... There would, we think, have to be some quite unforeseen change in this respect before Pilkington would deliberately set out to exploit its position of strength at the expense of the public interest.   (*Flat Glass 1968**)

(In 1990, however, the Restrictive Practices Court found that Pilkington was acting against the public interest by taking part in a large number of price-fixing agreements.)

In another case the Commission said:

> this is a merger which would lead to a substantial degree of additional concentration in an already highly concentrated market. We believe, however that, in the exceptional circumstances of the declining market which we have described, it is unlikely that a merged Bryant & May/Masters would raise prices unreasonably, or materially reduce the number of brands available, or the standards of service to customers.   (*Swedish Match/Alleghany 1987**).

(That belief was subsequently shown to have been mistaken, and price control was recommended in order to reduce Bryant and May's excessive profits (*Matches 1992**).)

In view of these disappointments, it seems possible that future promises of good behaviour will be treated more sceptically by the Competition Commission.

The European Commission, supported by the European Court of Justice, have taken a different approach. In the leading case which has already been referred to, the argument that it would be necessary to show some abusive exploitation, as distinct from a mere structural change in the organisation of the two enterprises, was specifically rejected by the Court (*Continental Can 1973*). The difference in this respect between the EU and UK approaches led the European

Commission, in two cases, to impose further or more stringent conditions upon mergers which had been cleared by the Monopolies and Mergers Commission (*BA/BCal 1987, Minorco/ConsGold 1989*).

B Jurisdiction and the selection of cases

The number of mergers which are ruled upon by the competition authorities is very small in proportion to their total incidence. The following sections of this chapter review the treatment by the authorities of some specific issues arising in those merger cases. Of more interest to most business executives, however, are the characteristics of those mergers which escape regulation, either because they do not fall within its jurisdiction, or because they are excluded by the selection procedures adopted by the authorities.

All mergers having a *community dimension*[7] must be notified to the European Commission. Under British legislation, there is no requirement to notify a merger to the Office of Fair Trading, although it may save time to do so.[8] There is a presumption under both EU and UK procedures that a merger leading to a combined market-share[9] of less than 25 per cent will be cleared without formal investigation.

The European Commission's jurisdiction

The Commission normally has jurisdiction over all mergers that have a community dimension. It may, however, refer a qualifying merger to the competition authority of a member state where a problem of market dominance arises in a distinct market, within that member state, which is isolated from the rest of the Community, for example, by high transport costs. The Commission referred a merger involving Tarmac and Steetley to the UK authorities at their request, although it satisfied the criteria for EU jurisdiction, because it would have given the combined firm control of almost 80 per cent of brickmaking capacity in the Northwest of England. (That merger would have had no effects outside the UK, however, despite Steetley's large French interests.)

In exceptional circumstances, a member country may be able to exclude a qualifying merger from the Commission's jurisdiction. The application of the regulation is stated to be without prejudice to Article 23 of the Treaty and not to prevent member states from taking

---

[7] Defined on p. 27.
[8] As noted on p. 49.
[9] The choice of market definition for this pupose is important: see p. 62.

appropriate measures to protect legitimate interests other than those pursued by the regulation.[10] The UK government considered British Aerospace's 1994 bid for VSEL to fall within that category because it affected national security interests, and instructed British Aerospace not to notify the bid to the Commission. That contention was accepted by the European Commission as regards the military aspects of the merger, but its nonmilitary aspects were examined and cleared, following the Commission's normal merger procedures. The Commission indicated,[11] however, that exemption from notification in respect even of military activities would not have been accepted had there been more than slight effects in other member states.

United Kingdom merger jurisdiction

UK jurisdiction applies to mergers which satisfy either the share of supply criterion or the assets test of the Fair Trading Act.[12] It is limited, however, by the rule[13] that no member state shall apply its national legislation on competition to any consideration that has a Community dimension. Although no merger should fall within both jurisdictions, questions of definition may create some uncertainty as to which jurisdiction is to prevail.[14]

The Scope of the definition of a merger

Jurisdiction is not confined to mergers in which more than 50 per cent of a company's shares are acquired. It is sufficient under British law that there should be an ability to exert a material influence upon policy. The Office of Fair Trading advise that:

> a shareholding of 25% or more generally enables the holder to block special resolutions; consequently, this proportion is likely to be seen as automatically conferring the ability materially to influence policy – even when all the remaining shares are held by only one person. But the OFT may examine any case where there is a shareholding of 15% or more in order to see whether the holder might be able materially to influence the company's policy, while, very occasionally, a holding of less than 15% could also attract scrutiny.... A

[10] Rehearsal 28 and Article 21(3) of Regulation 4064/89.
[11] Comp Rep. 1994, p. 219.
[12] See p. 28.
[13] Article 21(2) Regulation 4064/89.
[14] The Director-General has advised companies who are in doubt to notify both authorities in order to avoid delay.

'controlling interest' generally means a shareholding carrying more than 50% of the voting rights in a company. Only one shareholder can have a controlling interest but it is not uncommon for a company to be subject to the control (in the wider sense) of two or more major shareholders at the same time in a joint venture, for instance....[15]

The ability to influence policy by means of a successful threat to withdraw support was considered to confer material influence in a case involving the acquisition of a 20 per cent shareholding (*Stagecoach/Mainline 1995*). Also, a transfer of assets may be deemed to constitute a qualifying merger, even if the business concerned is not transferred to the acquiring firm as a going concern. Because of the continued operation of bus services from an acquired depot, that acquisition was considered to qualify although it would have been possible – though not commercially sensible – to operate the services without the depot (*Stagecoach/Lancaster City 1993*).

Under EU merger law, control is deemed to be constituted by:

rights or contracts which confer decisive influence on the composition, voting or decisions of the organs of an undertaking.[16]

In one case a 19 per cent holding combined with a right to appoint the chairman and the chief executive was held to constitute control (*CCIE/GTE 1992*). Also, in the case of joint ventures, control may be conferred by contracts concerning the running of the business.[17] The possibility of joint control is recognised when there are equal shareholdings or when joint consent is required for important decisions.

C   The treatment of horizontal mergers

Market power and concentration

Although the purpose of merger control is to limit the acquisition of market power, the authorities do not in practice intervene unless a notional threshold is exceeded. A broad indication of that threshold is provided by a qualified presumption that the acquisition of market shares greater than 40 per cent will be prohibited. The qualifications

[15] OFT Mergers guide – see Appendix 2.
[16] Article 3(3) of the merger regulation.
[17] Commission Notice OJ C 203 of 14/8/1990.

are, however, important. They arise from the limited extent to which market power is measured by market share.[18]

Among important qualifying factors are the degree of *concentration*[19] in the market, and the extent to which it would be increased by the merger. (The US merger guidelines use concentration measures to classify mergers, but there are no concentration thresholds in the UK and EU guidelines.) In highly concentrated markets, mergers leading to market shares well below 40 per cent have normally been prohibited by both the UK and the EU authorities.[20] In the context of the concentrated and vertically integrated UK beer market, for example, a market-share limit of 15 per cent has been proposed – although not implemented (*Elders/Grand Met 1990**). However, the authorities have taken a more permissive attitude toward high market-shares in markets characterised by vigorous competition, even where there are high levels of concentration. A merger which raised the already high level of concentration in the market for recorded music was cleared because there was vigorous competition in that market (*Thorn EMI/Virgin 1992**) and the existence of a strong and active competitor was a consideration which influenced the clearance of a food industry merger leading to a combined market share of 90 per cent (*Hillsdown/Associated British Foods 1992*). And the European Commission have stated that high market shares in high-growth markets involving modern technology do not, in any case, necessarily indicate undesirable market power (*Digital/Phillips 1991*).

The second-best

According to the theory of the second-best,[21] however, action to prevent an increase in concentration may not be the preferred option if the market is already highly concentrated. If a return to a fully competitive environment is not feasible, the second-best option may be to allow the development of countervailing market power.

A merger between the second- and third-largest firms in the industry may be the best way of restraining the power of the market leader – provided that there is no prospect of tacit collusion with the market leader.

Examples of the authorities' treatment of that consideration include:

[18] See pp. 63–8.
[19] Measures of concentration are defined in Appendix 1.
[20] See Neven, Nuttall & Seabright 1993 for an analysis of EU decisions by Herfindahl Index.
[21] Also discussed on p. 7.

- clearance of a merger between two manufacturers, which gave them a 60 per cent share of the market for plain biscuits (*Nabisco/Huntley & Palmer 1982**);
- clearance of a merger between food groups with wholesaling and retailing interests (*Linfood/Fitch Lovell 1983**);
- and of a further such merger (*Dee/Booker McConnell 1985**);
- prohibition of a proposed merger between two brewers, which would have given them a combined market share comparable with the market leader (at about 40 per cent), because of doubts that they would compete effectively with the market leader (*Elders/Scottish & Newcastle 1989*).

That consideration may also have been the reason for not referring the supermarket mergers of Argyll with Safeway and Dee with Fine Fare.

Buying power

Another form of countervailing power may be supplied by the buying power of large customers and examples of cases in which that consideration has influenced merger decisions have already been listed.[22]

Entry prospects

The most important influence upon the treatment of mergers has, however, been the prospects of entry, as was illustrated by the observation that in only one out of 22 cases examined by the Monopolies and Mergers Commission between 1980 and 1986 was there an adverse finding in the absence of entry barriers. Some mergers have been cleared because market shares were reduced by supply-side substitution[23] generated by entry prospects, while others have been cleared on the grounds that entry prospects offset the effects of high market shares.[24]

Rationalisation

It has sometimes been argued that, since a firm could not survive without a proposed merger, the merger would serve to preserve competitive capacity. On other occasions it has also been argued that the proposed merger would confer a net benefit by enabling excess capacity to be removed. The Commission have made the following statement concerning the formation of crisis cartels:

[22] On p. 73.
[23] Defined on p. 66.
[24] Some of which are listed on p. 71.

The Commission may be able to condone agreements in restraint of competition which relate to a sector as a whole, provided that they are aimed solely at achieving a coordinated reduction of overcapacity, and do not otherwise restrict decision-making by the firms involved. The necessary structural reorganisation must not be achieved by unsuitable means such as price-fixing or quota agreements...The Commission must be satisfied that after the reorganisation is complete there will still be a sufficient number of Community manufacturers left to maintain effective competition.[25]

Practical examples of the authorities' treatment of rationalisation arguments include the following:[26]

- the approval of an agreement among 16 producers to close seven plants to counter overcapacity in the Dutch building-brick industry;[27]
- the clearance of a merger between the only two cross-channel hovercraft operators on the grounds that they might otherwise be forced to abandon hovercraft operations (*British Rail/HoverLloyd 1981**);
- the clearance of a merger leading to a 90 per cent market share, on the grounds that the raspberry operations of one of the companies would otherwise have been closed (*Hillsdown/Associated British Foods 1992**);
- the prohibition of a merger between ferry companies which would have given them a 71 per cent market share, on the grounds that it was not the best way of dealing with excess capacity (*European Ferries/ Sealink 1981**);
- the subsequent clearance of a further merger leading to a 50 per cent market share in the same industry, in view of strong entry prospects (*P&O/European Ferries 1986**);
- the clearance (subject to price undertakings) of a merger of two Scottish dairies on the grounds that without it, one of them was unlikely to survive (*Robert Wiseman/Scottish Pride 1996**);
- the clearance of a bus merger yielding a 63 per cent market share, because of the conviction that the smaller firm could not have survived independently (and because of entry prospects in the longer term) (*Stagecoach/Chesterfield 1996**).

[25] Competition Report No. 23, 1993.
[26] * indicates reports of the former MMC, which were not intended to create precedents.
[27] Commission press release IP/941353 of 2/5/94.

D Vertical and conglomerate mergers

Vertical issues[28]

The merger of a dominant firm with one of its suppliers raises the possibility that it may manipulate its 'upstream' market to the detriment of its competitors. It is unlikely to be able to do so, however, unless it acquires a substantial share of that market. The market share acquired has been found to be too small to endanger competition in a number of cases examined by the European Commission (such as *AT&T/NCR 1991* and *Mitsubishi/UCAR 1991*). In the UK, permission for a telephone company to acquire a telephone manufacturer was made subject to a statutory undertaking limiting the UK market share of the equipment (*BT/ Mitel 1986*). The acquisition of Britain's largest sugar refiner by its largest sugar merchant was made subject to the cessation by the merchant of trading in sugar from a competing refiner and the maintenance of the refiner as a separate subsidiary with its own accounts (*Berisford/British Sugar 1981*).

It is similarly possible that the 'downstream' acquisition of a sales outlet could be used to restrict competition – but with the same qualification concerning downstream market share. The merger of a packaging company with an aluminium company was permitted by the European Commission because 40 per cent of the packaging market was met by other suppliers and there were other vertically integrated aluminium companies in that market (*Viag/Continental Can 1991*). Similarly, the acquisition of a distributor by a steel producer was cleared because a sufficient number of independent distributors remained (*ASD/ Usinor 1991*). The Monopolies and Mergers Commission cleared a merger between two car-rental firms in one of which a car manufacturer had an interest, on the basis of assurances that the manufacturer's cars would not be supplied to it on preferential terms (*Europcar/Godfrey Davis 1981*).

Conglomerate mergers

Mergers can sometimes raise competition issues even when there is no apparent horizontal or vertical integration. The Monopolies and Mergers Commission have referred to the dangers of cross-subsidisation and the loss of financial information (*Blue Circle/Armitage Shanks 1980*) but have never blocked a conglomerate merger.

---

[28] The wider question of vertical restraints is dealt with in Chapter 7.

Where the merging firms produce complementary products, there is a further risk that they may restrict competition by marketing their products together as an integrated system. That possibility has been examined but rejected in several cases considered by the European Commission (e.g. *Matsushita/ MCA 1991* and *TetraPak/Alfa Laval 1991*).

E Joint ventures

Joint ventures have some of the characteristics of mergers, and some of the characteristics of restrictive agreements. Until the Competition Act 1998 came into force, they were dealt with in the UK under the Restrictive Trade Practices Act 1976. The Office of Fair Trading provided the following guidance concerning the circumstances under which action before the court could be avoided:

Joint ventures commonly include restrictions on the parent companies not to compete with the joint venture. In considering such restrictions, the Office looks for clear evidence of competition in the relevant market from other suppliers or from other substitute goods or services and that no evidence of possible detriments to third parties has been forthcoming. A number of such joint venture agreements which in their original form were thought to contain significant restrictions have been modified to make them suitable for a representation to the Secretary of State. Joint venture agreements to promote research and development may also be suitable for a representation if the Office is satisfied that, without the restrictions they contain, the development would not take place.

The sanctioning of a joint venture usually implies the acceptance of those restrictions which are necessary to enable the parent companies to recover their initial investment. The treatment of restrictions upon the parent companies not to compete with the joint venture has been a matter of some controversy, however. If the activities to be performed by the joint venture would not otherwise take place, it would seem illogical to suggest that competition is restricted by *prior* undertakings not to compete with it. If, however, the authorities were to consider only the effects upon competition *after* the joint venture had been set up, they could then regard such undertakings as restrictive.[29]

[29] Some say DGIV has mistakenly taken the latter *ex post* view (Korah 1997, p 209).

EU legislation draws a procedural distinction between concentrative and cooperative joint ventures, dealing with the former under its mergers legislation, and dealing with the latter as agreements under the more stringent requirements of Article 81. Concentrative joint ventures were originally defined for the purpose as not giving rise to coordination with and between the partners, as well as being *full-function*. The former requirement has since been dropped (although the Commission have retained the option of examining any coordinating aspects and, if necessary, of initiating second-stage action under Article 81.) A joint venture is now considered to be *full-function*, and therefore subject to the merger regulation, if it:

> performs on a lasting basis all the functions of an autonomous economic entity, and has all the necessary resources to perform those functions, in terms of funding, staff and tangible and intangible assets.

Examples[30] of the Commission's interpretation of this rule include:

- the exclusion of a joint venture for the production of welded steel sheet because it would be wholly dependent upon its parents for raw materials and would not be free to negotiate prices with them;
- the inclusion of a joint venture for the production of lighting equipment, despite the fact that its products would be sold to its parents during its start-up period;
- the inclusion also of a joint venture for the manufacture of veterinary products, even though some of its raw materials would be supplied by its parents and although it would, for a time, be an exclusive distributor of some of the products of one of its parents;
- the decision to disregard links of minor importance and the fact that some of its plants were on its parents' sites and therefore to include a joint venture between two chemical companies for the upstream production of polythene (despite some concern about the possibility that it might lead to coordination of its parents' activities);
- the interpretation of a seven-year period of life as satisfying the requirement that the arrangement 'performs on lasting basis...'.

In making its appraisal, the Commission is now required to take into account the following *spillover* effects:

---

[30] These examples are described in more detail on pp. 185–9 of the XXVIIth Report on Competition Policy (1997) – see Appendix 2.

(i)   whether two or more parent companies retain to a significant extent activities in the same market as the joint venture or in a market which is downstream or upstream of that of the joint venture or in a neighbouring market closely related to this market, and

(ii)   whether the coordination which is the direct consequence of the joint venture affords the undertakings concerned the possibility of eliminating competition in respect of a substantial part of the products or services in question.[31]

Among the possible characteristics of a joint venture of either type which are likely to favour its clearance or exemption are:

(a)   the contribution by the partners of expertise which is likely to make for more effective competition in the joint venture's market;

(b)   the bringing together of complementary resources to make possible an activity which could not realistically be undertaken by either parent on its own;

(c)   the sharing of risks which are too great for the partners to bear individually;

(d)   the existence of effective competition in the parents' markets;

(e)   the absence in the agreement of unnecessary restrictions upon the competitive behaviour of the partners.

Possible obstacles to clearance include:

(f)   the control of a network of competing joint ventures, which would protect one of them against competition from the others;

(g)   agreements requiring exclusive dealing with the parents;

(h)   vertical links enabling the foreclosure of a market.

Joint ventures involving the setting-up of new organisations requiring substantial amounts of investment (termed *structural joint ventures*) are dealt with by an accelerated procedure under which comfort letters are issued within two months of notification unless the Commission has serious doubts of their compatibility with the Common Market.[32]

A limited class of joint ventures for R&D is exempted by Regulation 418/84, which also provides, under defined circumstances, for a limited period of commercial exploitation.

---

[31] Article 2(4) of the merger regulation 4064/89 as amended by Regulation 1310/97.

[32] See the Commission's XXIInd Report on Competition Policy (1992), points 122–4.

Practical examples of the generally permissive EU treatment of joint ventures, under Article 81 and under the merger regulation, include:

- the (exemption-type) clearance by comfort letter of the joint takeover of an Italian cruise operator by a British and an American cruise operator (under which it was agreed to restrict the parents' French and Italian operations) – on the grounds that the partners could be expected to use their expertise to improve the promotion of Mediterranean cruises and reduce their costs (*Carnival/Airtours 1997*);
- the negative clearance of a joint venture to operate alongside its parents in the Swedish internet access market on the grounds that – although one of its parents had a 25–40 per cent market share – the market was fast-growing and entry barriers were low (*Telia/Telenor 1998*);
- the negative clearance of each of two joint ventures which brought together complementary technology for the production of optical fibres; and the exemption of the resulting network of joint ventures, subject to the removal of a number of possibly restrictive features of the arrangement (*Optical Fibres 1986*);
- the clearance of joint ventures concerning satellite communications, in which some of the partners contributed nothing but finance, on the grounds that the project was too large to be financed by fewer firms (*Private Satellite Partners 1994*);
- the exemption, during a five-year launch period, of a joint venture for the R&D and production of cholesterol-reducing dairy products, parented by the dominant dairy products firms in Denmark and Sweden – but the exclusion from the exemption of the production by the joint venture of conventional dairy products (*Scandairy 1997*);
- the authorisation under the merger regulation of a joint venture which, as proposed, would have strengthened an already dominant position in the Danish soft-drinks market; but which, after some transfers and divestments, was considered to leave adequate prospects for the entry of competitors (*Coca Cola/Carlsberg 1997*);
- the prohibition of a joint venture which had been intended to rescue one of the partners from financial difficulties, but which would have given the two leading firms a 60 per cent share of the market for silicon carbide (*Saint Gobain/Wacker 1996*);
- the clearance of a proposed joint venture by two major oil companies for the refining and marketing of fuels and lubricants in view of strong local competition and competition from the other majors and in view of downstream over-capacity (*BP/Mobil 1996*);

- the prohibition of a joint venture to have been established between dominant companies in national cable and satellite TV markets, which would have established links between programme-production, transmission and retailing, and which, in the Commission's view, enable foreclosure of the Scandinavian satellite TV market (*Nordic Satellite Distribution 1995*).

F   Non-competition issues

Merger control is not exclusively concerned with the balance between competition loss and efficiency gain. Other considerations are stipulated in the Treaty of Rome.[33] In the UK, the wide scope of the public interest criteria[34] enables a virtually unlimited range of other issues to be taken into account.

Non-competition issues have only occasionally affected UK mergers control, however. Concern for the future of football was an issue affecting the blocking of the BSkyB bid for Manchester United in 1999, but there had been few other occasions in preceding years. The only plausible explanation for repeated inquiries into bids for the Harrods department store[35] seems to have been popular interest in the store and in the personality and management style of the bidder. Controversies about management style and performance are, of course, commonplace in contested bids, and there have been several cases in which they were the central issue in merger inquiries.[36] On several occasions,[37] the nationality of the bidder became the central issue, and nationalist sentiments appear to have influenced some other inquiries.[38] Among other non-competition issues which have arisen have included highly-leveraged bids, employment considerations and acquisitions by state-controlled overseas firms.

When there are rival bids of which one raises competition issues and the other does not, the decision whether to refer one or both may raise a dilemma. A decision to refer only the one that raises competition issues may seem inequitable. For example, when both Lloyds and HSBC bid for Midland Bank in 1983, HSBC won the contest simply because only the Lloyds bid was referred. The alternative of referring both bids was

---

[33]   Article 2 – quoted on p. 76.
[34]   The public interest criteria listed on p. 30.
[35]   *Lonrho/SUITS 1979*, and *Lonrho/House of Fraser 1981 and 1985*.
[36]   For example, *Taubman/Sotheby 1983* and *Lewis/Illingworth Morris 1983*.
[37]   For instance, *Kuwait/BP 1988*.
[38]   Such as *BA/BCal 1987*.

adopted in 1994 when both GEC and BAe bid for the submarine-maker VSEL, despite the lack of any overlap between the activities of BAe and VSEL.

The possibility of political intervention in support of a favoured domestic supplier has been a matter of concern on several occasions. It led the European Commission to impose more stringent conditions upon the BA/BCal merger than had been necessary to satisfy the UK authorities. And the Commission's 1991 prohibition of the proposed merger between ATR and de Havilland led to protests from the French and Italian governments and a hostile resolution by the European Parliament.

Generally speaking, however, attempts to introduce non-competition issues into merger control have either been unsuccessful or have produced patently unsatisfactory results, and that experience may have a discouraging influence on future conduct.

6
Pricing Policies

A   Introduction

While many of the commercial policies which are adopted by businesses may be pursued under conditions of secrecy, their pricing policies are necessarily open to inspection and analysis. It would seem that analysis of those policies offers the best prospect of detecting departures from competitive market conditions, and that their regulation should provide one of the most effective ways of limiting any resulting damage to the public interest. As this chapter will show, those appearances are deceptive. In fact, investigations of pricing policies and the prescription of remedies for abuse have often faced the competition authorities with some of their most serious conceptual and analytical problems.

The conceptual difficulties stem from the limitations of available competition theory. The propositions of 'mainstream' competition theory lead to straightforward rules as to what constitutes competitive pricing. But it is in this connection that the simplifications adopted by that theory are most apt to appear unrealistic. Rules which are derived for the pricing of risklessly developed undifferentiated products can hardly be expected to apply at all widely to today's markets. Alternative theories which are based upon more realistic assumptions indicate that economic efficiency could often be increased by departures from those rules, but those theories do not yield an alternative set of rules. Analytical problems often arise from the difficulties of allocating product costs, and of estimating the cost of capital.

This chapter examines the circumstances under which a company's pricing policies may fall within the jurisdiction of the competition authorities, and the treatment they may then be expected to receive. The following three sections are about their treatment of pricing policies which are used to augment or defend market power: Section B is about the avoidance of price competition by *price collusion*; Section C is about *price discrimination*; Section D deals with attempts to remove a competitor by *predatory pricing*.

The remaining two sections are about their treatment of allegedly abusive pricing polices by dominant companies: Section E is about the misuse of market power by *excessive pricing*, and Section F is concerned with *price regulation*.

B   Price collusion

Explicit price-fixing agreements, as an overt means of avoiding price competition, are certain of condemnation, and are consequently rare. But the authorities may also infer secret or tacit price-collusion from information exchange agreements, even if they do not have the explicit purpose of fixing prices. They may also infer such collusion from a similarity of price levels or price movements. Whether, in fact, they do so depends upon a variety of considerations. Where secret collusion is exposed by the investigation of the competition authorities, deterrent penalties are often imposed.

Information exchange

Action has sometimes been taken to prevent trade associations from exchanging commercially sensitive information likely to influence prices. That practice has been condemned, even when the exchange of information was not the result of an explicit agreement (*COBELPA 1977*). The European Commission recognises, however, that there are circumstances where there can be no objection to the exchange of information, even between competitors, and whether or not under the aegis of a trade association. The Commission has indicated in a Notice[1] the kind of information that may be exchanged without infringing Article 81(1). Examples are agreements which have as their sole object:

- the exchange of opinion or experience;
- joint market research;
- joint carrying out of comparative studies of enterprises or industries;
- joint preparation of statistics; cooperation in accounting matters;
- joint provision of credit guarantees; joint debt-collecting agencies;

[1] *Notice Concerning Agreements, Decisions & Concerted Practices*, OJ C 75/3 1968 & OJ C84 1968.

- joint business or tax consultant agencies; and
- joint implementation or placing of research and development projects.

The Commission has advised that an agreement for the collection of statistics is acceptable provided that:

- no individual information is distributed;
- the statistics are not discussed at meetings with competitors;
- information is disseminated without comments;
- the statistics do not cover prices, production forecasts or capacity utilisation forecasts.[2]

The publication of price lists for the information of customers is not, on its own, regarded as an infringement. The European Court's judgement on an arrangement by which members announced maximum prices quarterly in advance included the following statement:

> In this case, the communications arise from price announcements made to users. They constitute in themselves market behaviour, which does not lessen each undertaking's uncertainty as to the future attitude of its competitors. At the same time when each undertaking engages in such behaviour, it cannot be sure of the future conduct of the others. Accordingly, the system of quarterly price announcements...is not to be regarded as constituting in itself an infringement of Article 81(1). *(Woodpulp 1993)*

The attitudes of the authorities to such arrangements depend, moreover, upon the competitive nature of the market concerned. Concerning the activities of the trade association of the German steel industry, the European Commission observed that:

> It raised no objection to the exchange of sensitive information on dispersed markets. On the other hand, it did prohibit the exchange of data on all markets for flat products and on the markets for beams, sheet piling, and permanent way material and wire rod of stainless steel. These are concentrated markets characterised by low import penetration, stable trade flows between Member States and chronic overcapacity.... The decision is consistent with the Commission's

---

[2] CEPI-Cartonboard Comp. Rep. 1996, p. 127; also Cartonboard Cartel case of 13/7/94 OJ L 243.

practice, which has been upheld by the Court of First Instance, of viewing as anti-competitive any systems involving the exchange of sensitive, recent and individualised data on a concentrated market in homogeneous products. (*Wirtschaftsvereinigung Stahl 1997*)[3]

Other examples of the authorities' treatment of information exchange include:[4]

- the condemnation of the publication by the British Medical Association of guidelines for consultants' fees (*Medical Services 1994**);
- the condemnation – even in the absence of evidence of other anti-competitive practices – of a system of confidential information exchange between tractor manufacturers in a market dominated by four firms (*UK Tractor 1992*);
- the clearance of a cost-calculation system enabling individual trade-association members to determine prices on the basis of their own costs – but the *prohibition* of a list of recommended prices (*Fenex 1996*);
- the treatment as a concerted practice of meetings with competitors, the purposes of which included influencing pricing conduct (*Polypropylene 1991, Netherlands Construction 1992*);
- The imposition of a fine of 50 million ecu on four sugar manufacturers with a combined market share of 90 per cent in connection with the holding of a series of price-fixing meetings (*Sugar 1998*);[5]
- The clearance of the exchange of prices in an international payment system where the recipients were not direct competitors (*IBOS 1996*).

Parallel pricing

A prohibited concerted practice can be deemed to exist, even when there is no explicit communication between the parties concerned:

it is sufficient for an independent undertaking knowingly and of its own accord to adjust its behaviour in line with the wishes of another undertaking. (*Hasselblad 1982*)

The European Court has ruled that the occurrence of parallel prices may under some circumstances be regarded as strong evidence of a concerted practice, namely when:

[3] As reported in the 1997 Competition Report.
[4] * indicates cases of the former Monopolies and Mergers Commission, which were not intended to set precedents.
[5] Cancelled on appeal.

it leads to conditions of competition which do not correspond to the normal conditions of the market...especially where the parallel behaviour is such as to permit the parties to seek price equilibrium at a different level from that which would have resulted from competition.   (*Dyestuffs 1972*)

But in a later judgement, the Court ruled that:

parallel conduct cannot be regarded as furnishing proof of concertation unless concertation constitutes the only possible explanation of such conduct.   (*Woodpulp 1993*)

Examples of the authorities' attitudes to similarities of prices and price movements include:

- condemnation, in view of wide differences in the suppliers' costs (*White Salt 1986**)
- approval, when suppliers offered competitive discounts (*Ceramic Sanitaryware 1978**, *Insulated Wires and Cables 1979**, *Steel Wire Fencing 1987**) – but not when the discounts were confined to large customers (*Concrete Roofing Tiles 1981**)
- the European Court's judgement that the mere fact that, in a concentrated market, a few firms take account of each other's prices does not amount to a concerted practice (*Suiker Unie 1976*)
- the finding that parallel price-movements of a wide range of products which could be observed in different national markets could not be explained except by collusion because each market was dominated by a local supplier (*Dyestuffs 1972*)

C Price discrimination

Price discrimination is prohibited under British and Community law, both as part of a restrictive agreement and as abuse of a dominant position, as being a practice of:

applying dissimilar conditions to equivalent transactions with other trading parties, thereby placing them at a competitive disadvantage.

Similar prohibitions occur in the United States Robinson–Patman Act.
    Most of the investigations of price discrimination by the competition authorities have arisen in connection with their investigations of other

policies. It has figured – for example, in the form of loyalty rebates – in their treatment of attempts by manufacturers to influence retailers,[6] and it has sometimes formed part of alleged predatory pricing.[7] However, there has been little in the way of precedent to indicate their attitude to price discrimination as part of normal commercial practice. But in view of the importance which they attach to the concept of the single market, the European Commission are certain to prohibit price discrimination as between the national markets of member states.

Geographical price discrimination was condemned by the European Court in a case in which a supplier of bananas related prices charged to retailers to the relative levels of demand in different countries:

> these discriminatory prices, which varied according to the circumstances of member states, were just so many obstacles to the free movement of goods.

and the Court raised a second objection:

> the mechanisms of the market are adversely affected if the price is calculated...taking into account the law of supply and demand as between the vendor and ultimate consumer, and not as between the vendor and the purchaser.
> (*United Brands 1978*)

Other cases in which geographical price discrimination has been condemned include *Pittsburg Corning 1972*, *Kodak 1970* and *Distillers 1980*. Non-geographical price discrimination has also been condemned.

These judgements must, however, be regarded as controversial in view of persuasive arguments[8] that the prohibition of price discrimination raises a danger of *false positive*[9] diagnosis, and even of eliminating bargaining-type competition under circumstances where it is the only type of competition available.

The Office of Fair Trading have noted that:

> Price discrimination...might be objectively justified in industries where there are large fixed costs and low marginal costs (the cost

---

[6] Covered in Chapter 7 below.
[7] See section D of this chapter.
[8] For example, the US Dept of Justice *Report on the Robinson–Patman Act*, 1977.
[9] The diagnosis of a detriment where none exists.

of supplying each additional unit of output is very small compared to the initial investment to set up the business). This is often the case in utility industries. In most markets, undertakings are normally expected to set prices equal to their marginal cost, but in such industries, an undertaking which did so would never be able to recover its fixed costs. It may therefore be more efficient to set higher prices to customers with a higher willingness to pay. In general, price discrimination will not be an abuse in such industries if it leads to higher levels of output than an undertaking could achieve by charging every customer the same price.[10]

D   Predatory pricing

There is an even greater danger of a false positive diagnosis of allegations of predatory pricing because of the similarity of the symptoms to those of successful competition. An accusation of predatory pricing from an unsuccessful rival is often deserving of a Mandy Rice-Davis response,[11] but although genuine cases are uncommon, the practice has been successfully employed to deter or eliminate competition.

Predatory pricing can be regarded as a particular case of the more general concept of *predation*, which has been defined as:

> the acceptance of losses in a particular market which are deliberately incurred in order to eliminate a specific competitor, so that supranormal profits can be earned in the future, either in the same or in other markets   (*Thamesway 1993*)

As a commercial strategy, predatory pricing is likely to be attractive only under rather special conditions. Obviously, the predator must have considerable market power and a 'deep pocket', but there are other considerations. It is easier to practise if the target company operates in an isolated market segment, so that the predator need not reduce its prices in other market segments. It carries a bigger payoff if, by establishing a reputation for the successful destruction of rivals, it deters the entry of new competitors into that or other market segments. Under the right conditions, it can be effective in eliminating a rival's resistance to a takeover bid.

---

[10] OFT guides to the Competition Act *The Chapter II Prohibition*, see Appendix 2.
[11] *'Well, he would, wouldn't he?'*

Cost-based criteria: the Areeda–Turner rule

With a view to excluding misguided investigations, American competition lawyers[12] have put forward the criteria that:

- only if prices are set below *short-run marginal costs*[13] should they be presumed to be predatory: and that,
- in view of the difficulty of measuring marginal costs, *average variable cost*[14] is a generally acceptable surrogate.

The British and European Union competition authorities have generally considered that rule to be too permissive. Prices below average variable costs are generally[15] taken as conclusive proof of predation, but the possibility of predation is not excluded by prices above that level. The Office of Fair Trading have taken the view[16] that prices may be predatory even if they exceed short-run marginal costs but are less than average total cost – but that a pricing policy which does not cover capital and overhead cost cannot be presumed to be predatory. Failure to recover *avoidable costs*[17] is indicative of predation. The European Commission have pointed out that the use of short-run rather than long-run costs takes inadequate account of the strategic nature of predation. They have gone further to state that even pricing above full costs can be anti-competitive:

> the important element is the rival's assessment of the aggressor's determination to frustrate its expectations, for example as to its rate of growth or attainable profit margins, rather than whether or not the dominant firm covers its own costs. There can thus be an anti-competitive aspect to price-cutting whether or not the aggressor sets its prices above or below its own costs.   (*ECS/AKZO 1986*)

Cost-based criteria were unsuccessfully used by the defence in that case and in *Concrete Roofing Tiles 1981*.

---

[12] Areeda and Turner 1975 and 1978.
[13] The cost of increasing output by one unit when that does not require an increase in productive capacity.
[14] The average cost per unit, excluding costs which remain constant in the short- to medium-term.
[15] With the exceptions noted below.
[16] *Becton Dickinson 1988*.
[17] Avoidable by ceasing the operation, excluding costs incurred in common with other operations, and sunk costs not incurred for the purposes of predation.

Behavioural criteria

The Office of Fair Trading focuses on three types of evidence:[18]

- whether the structure and characteristics of the market and the alleged predator are such as to make predation a sensible and feasible business strategy;
- whether the alleged predator incurs losses arising from that course of conduct; and,
- what the intentions of the alleged predator are – taking into account any relevant evidence of its behaviour in other markets.

A pricing policy which is the result of a mistake, or which has an objective justification other than the elimination of a competitor will not be deemed predatory. Examples[19] include:

- *loss leading* in which the price reduction increases the sales of complementary products;
- *promotions* which are brief and infrequent;
- *network effects* under which the costs of selective price-cutting can be recovered from customers who benefit from expansion of the network;
- *mistaken profit expectations* because of ill-judged market entry or unexpected cost increases;
- *incrementally profitable price reductions* where the losses incurred are offset by increased profits from complementary activities.

Practical applications

Cases involving predatory pricing by British companies were rare during the early years of British competition policy. It arose in only about a dozen references to the Monopolies and Mergers Commission between 1950 and 1980. In the 1980s and 1990s, however, with the deregulation of the bus services in the 1980s, it figured widely in mergers cases and in investigations of uncompetitive practices by the Office of Fair Trading. The proliferation of cases during that period can be accounted for partly by the lack of penalties at that time, and partly by the fact that investigations often took place after the objective of the predation had been largely[20] achieved.

[18] As noted in *Thamesway 1993*.
[19] Abridged from the OFT guide *Assessment of Individual Agreements and Practices*.
[20] Not entirely, since limited price controls were applied as noted in section F of this chapter.

The early cases were relatively straightforward because they dealt with established predatory practices in heavily cartelised industries (*Matches 1953* and *Industrial Gases 1956*). Certainty of condemnation was subsequently established in other cases where intent could either be ascertained from the predator's records or confidently inferred from the magnitude or the targeting of the price cuts (e.g. *Librium and Valium 1973*, *Contraceptive Sheaths 1975*, *Gas 1988*).

Among the findings in less straightforward cases were:

- the condemnation of deep selective discounting by a monopoly supplier on the grounds that 'in the circumstances of this industry' it created an entry barrier, despite the acceptance that the prices in question were not below average variable cost, and that the objective was not to eliminate a competitor at all costs (*Concrete Roofing Tiles 1981**);

- the condemnation – in an extremely unusual case – of a monopolist's practice of offering his suppliers unreasonably high prices in order to deprive competitors of raw materials (*Animal Waste 1985**);

- the clearance – after extensive analysis – of the pricing policies of a major supplier of hypodermic needles to the National Health Service because it was considered unlikely that a predatory pricing strategy could succeed, and in the absence of any evidence of intent (*Becton Dickinson 1988*);

- the condemnation of the carrying out of threats to undercut a competitor's prices if he did not withdraw from the market, even though the prices charged satisfied the Areeda–Turner criteria (*ECS/AKZO 1986*);

- the clearance of the loss-making prices of electricity showrooms in view of the limited market power of the electricity companies in markets which were not tightly segmented and in which entry barriers were low, so that predatory pricing was unlikely to be successful (*Regional Electricity Companies 1993*);

- criticism of the pricing policy of an electricity board on the grounds that, although their prices were in line with their competitors, they were out of line with their costs (*London Electricity Board 1983*);

- the clearance of a price-cutting bus operation on the grounds that the operator's losses had not been increased by the price cuts and that the following increases in the rival company's losses were due to other factors (*Thamesway 1993*);

- the condemnation of a successful price-cutting campaign by a subsidiary of one of the largest bus groups (Stagecoach) which caused substantial losses to the price cutter and to its rival, and which contributed to Stagecoach's reputation for successful predation (*Fife Scottish 1994*).

E   Excessive pricing

Until recently, the principal source of case law on the subject of excessive pricing has been the score or so of cases examined by the former Monopolies and Mergers Commission over a 40-year period. In recent years, however, more intensive investigation of pricing levels resulted from calls upon that body to rule upon the pricing of the public utilities. It is likely that the methods developed as a result of those investigations will be adapted to investigations under the Competition Act of public utilities and, for consistency, of other dominant firms.

The European Commission, on the other hand, have declared their intention of leaving the regulation of the pricing policies of the public utilities as far as possible to the national authorities. Consequently, the common ground that exists between domestic and Community practice over most aspects of competition policy may not extend to excessive pricing. The different – though not necessarily incompatible – past treatments of the topic by the UK and the EU authorities must therefore be examined separately.

The EU approach

Article 82 of the Treaty of Amsterdam[21] explicitly prohibits 'imposing unfair purchasing or selling prices' by a dominant firm, but gives no guidance as to what is deemed to be an unfair price. In an early case, the European Court ruled[22] that a price is to be deemed excessive if it is 'excessive in relation to the economic value of the service provided'. In a subsequent case,[23] the Court held that:

> an excess could, inter alia, be determined objectively if it were possible for it to be calculated by making a comparison between the selling price of the product in question and its cost of production,

and later that

> when an undertaking holding a dominant position imposes scales of fees for its services which are appreciably higher than those charged

---

[21] Formerly Article 86 of the Treaty of Rome.
[22] *General Motors Continental 1976*.
[23] *United Brands 1978*.

in other Member States and where a comparison of the fee levels has been made on a consistent basis, that difference must be regarded as indicative of an abuse of a dominant position. In such a case, it is for the undertaking in question to justify the difference by reference to objective dissimilarities between the situation in the Member States concerned and the situation prevailing in all the other Member States.[24]

The assumption has been adopted that a price is highly likely to be abusive if it exceeds those found in comparable markets by more than 100 per cent, and investigations may be necessary for smaller differences.[25]

Examples of the Commission's use of these alternative approaches include:

- the investigation, with the help of accounting consultants, of the costs of publishing telephone directories, resulting in a 90 per cent price reduction (*Belgacom 1997*);
- a comparative market study of telephone tariffs leading to reductions of 38–78 per cent (*Deutsche Telekom 1998*).

The UK approach

The Office of Fair Trading has advised[26] that

the Director General expects to follow the European Commission and be cautious in finding excessive prices, in themselves, to be an abuse. He will be mindful of the need not to interfere in natural market mechanisms where high prices will encourage new entry and thereby serve to increase competition. Excessive prices are likely to be regarded as an abuse only in markets where an undertaking is so dominant and new entry so unlikely, that the undertaking is in a position similar to a natural monopoly and it is clear that high profits will not stimulate successful new entry.

Cost-related pricing

The UK authorities have also attempted to identify excessive prices by comparison with production costs. This was done successfully in an

[24] *Bodson 1988.*
[25] See Haag and Klotz 1998.
[26] OFT guide to the Competition Act *The Chapter II Prohibition* (see Appendix 2).

early case in which production costs were divulged by the supplier (*Librium and Valium 1973*). That approach was generally impracticable, however, because of the absence of powers to demand such information, prior to the coming into force of the 1998 Competition Act. There may now be a return to that approach. It has been suggested that pricing by dominant multi-product firms may in future be judged against the *stand-alone costs*[27] of each product.

Cost information was available to the Monopolies and Mergers Commission in their dealings with the public utilities before privatisation, and cost-based pricing was advocated in the following terms:

> On the grounds of economic efficiency, a consumer should normally be faced, in making his decision how much to consume, with the true resource cost he imposes on the system. Conventionally, this implies some form of marginal cost pricing. However, long- and short-run marginal costs differ widely. Much expenditure is once-for-all capital expenditure, the costs of operating the resulting capacity being much less than that of setting it up in the first place. Once the system has been laid down, there is no straightforward argument for including more than the operating costs in marginal cost for pricing purposes, costs of past investment being regarded as 'bygones'. Indeed, if capacity is under-utilised, it is clearly reasonable to set prices at a low level (provided that operating costs are covered) in order to increase capacity utilisation. However, if demand presses on capacity, or promises to do so shortly, then the price needs to include the unit cost of prospective additions to capacity. This will ensure that the cost of additional capacity will only be incurred in response to a demonstration by consumers that they are prepared to defray the whole of it.[28]

The Commission were critical of departures from those principles in the levying of standing charges for electricity (*SSEB 1986*), for off-peak charges for rail travel (*British Rail 1987*) and for the pricing of interruptible supplies (*Gas 1988*).

It has been noted, however, that to set prices equal to marginal costs would be commercially impracticable in cases in which it would lead to accounting losses, because it would not provide for the recovery of fixed costs.

---

[27] See the OFT's definition: at Appendix 1.
[28] *Severn-Trent 1981.*

Acceptable rates of return

The Commission's attitude to the prices charged by private-sector monopolies at about that time was determined mainly by their profit rates. They issued no guidance at that time as to what profit rates they deemed to be acceptable, but a survey of cases summarised in the Annex to this chapter suggests that prices were unlikely to have been found excessive unless rates of return were at least 50 per cent above the national average, and that rates of more than twice the average could escape condemnation in the absence of aggravating circumstances. In competitive markets with low entry barriers, the Commission were content to ascribe even exceptionally high profit rates to superior efficiency (as in the case of Nestlé in *Soluble Coffee 1991*). Where, on the other hand, an efficient supplier earns high profits by following the price leadership of a less efficient competitor, those profits have been attributed to excessive pricing (*White Salt 1986*).

The concept of an acceptable rate of return was gradually forced upon the Commission in the course of a series of references,[29] in which the Commission were required to resolve disputes between the newly-privatised public utilities and their regulators during the 1990s. The reports on those references provide the best available guide to future practice in this respect. In them, the Commission stipulate that prices should be such as to provide existing shareholders with reasonable, but not excessive, returns the operative criterion being that the companies' prices should be such as to enable them to attract new investment. This led to intensive studies of the *cost of capital* to the companies concerned, taking account of the riskiness of the activities undertaken. The *Capital Asset Pricing Model* was found to provide an analytically coherent method of estimating the cost of capital, but it was found to give rise to a wide range of uncertainties arising from the expert judgements which it requires. In one case, for example, it yielded a range from 4 per cent to over 10 per cent (*Gas 1993*) and in another, the Commission's judgement – following an extensive analysis by a variety of different methods – was challenged by the industry's Regulator (*Northern Ireland Electricity 1997*).

The Office of Fair Trading have also referred to the possibility of using a calculation of the *Certainty Equivalent Accounting Rate of Return* (CARR) as proposed in Graham and Steele 1997.

[29] *Gas 1993, Scottish Hydroelectric 1995, BAA 1996, Northern Ireland Electricity 1997*, Manchester Airport 1997.

The experience gained in connection with the pricing policies of the public utilities has occasionally been read across to investigations of other monopoly companies. In relation to the pricing policies of a monopoly ferry operator (reported to be offering passengers the world's most expensive sea-passage) the Commission commented:

> A return on capital employed on depreciated replacement cost of about 12 per cent in 1990 is somewhat above the level which has been adopted in the regulation of low-risk public utilities and, indeed, somewhat above those for the economy as a whole (the current cost accounting rate of return for all industrial and commercial companies in the UK in 1990 was 10 per cent – but the average over the previous five years was 7.8 per cent)...12 per cent is substantially toward the upper limit for a company enjoying such a strong market position – but not so high as to be regarded as excessive or to justify regulatory intervention.   (*Cross-Solent Ferries 1992*)

F   Price regulation

Price regulation is the obvious remedy for predatory pricing and for excessive pricing, but it has been employed with some reluctance. The authorities have been concerned both with the danger of making a false positive diagnosis and with the danger of imposing a remedy that is worse than the disease. They have had, on the other hand, to take account of public concern with matters of equity. In the UK and elsewhere in Europe, the transfers of the market power of the public utilities from governments to commercial undertakings have been on the explicit understanding that their pricing policies would be regulated.

As a remedy, price regulation has two inherent disadvantages. Where the possibility of competition remains, it has the disadvantage of removing the incentive for entry. And whether or not there is such a possibility, it has the disadvantage of removing the incentive for innovation, investment and efficient management. In addition, there may be serious incidental disadvantages arising from the difficulty of forecasting the relevant developments in the market and in the technology.

The European Commission have said that they propose to leave the regulation of public utilities to the national authorities, and their interventions have taken the form of the acceptance of price reductions proposed by the companies. In the UK, the regulation of each public utility is undertaken jointly by the appointed Regulator and the

Director General of Fair Trading, with appeals to the Competition Commission.

The form of price regulation recommended by the former Monopolies and Mergers Commission was usually stated in simple terms, such as 'no price increases for three years, followed by a pricing review'. The utilities regulators, however, have adopted formulae intended to allow for inflation and for the productivity increases which they deemed it reasonable to expect (usually referred to as 'RPI minus x'). The permitted increases have in some cases been related to the weighted average of a 'basket' of tariffs, and in other cases to the total revenue yield per unit of output. Each method has drawbacks.[30]

[30] The basket method can be evaded by concentrating price increases upon the fastest-growing markets; the revenue-yield method by reducing output-related charges and increasing standing charges.

Annex 6.1: MMC assessments of profits

Assessments of profits in a selection of the reports of the Monopolies and Mergers Commission 1980–94

Rates of return on capital[1] *for 5–6 years preceding the inquiry*[2,3]
(Annual, averages in parentheses)
Some cases in which prices were found not to be excessive

A	–	14	2	17	23	24	(17)	
B	–	16	6	9	9	45	(17)	Ease of entry
C	–	15	25	22	25	16	(19)	
D	14	30	24	15	18	18	(20)	
E	24	28	13	18	37	27	(25)	
F	–	34	35	47	39	40	(39)	
G	68	59	55	68	80	68	(66)	Ease of entry
H	–	50	65	99	118	114	(89)	Competitive market

Some cases in which prices were found to be excessive

I(a)	37	14	17	15	26	33	(24)	as supplied to MMC
(b)	64	29	29	20	30	40	(35)	as supplied to OFT
J	36	19	25	46	51	64	(40)	Complex monopoly
K	–	47	37	44	51	27	(41)	
L	46	45	53	45	35	32	(43)	Parallel pricing
M	–	54	49	47	34	32	(43)	Predatory pricing
N	61	78	69	68	91	62	(72)	Low-risk product
O	102	85	94	80	67	58	(81)	Low entry prospects

Notes

1 Case index:

A	*Contraceptive Sheaths 1994*	I	*Contraceptive Sheaths 1982*
B	*Animal Waste 1985*	J	*Roadside Advertising 1981*
C	*Liquefied Petroleum Gas 1981*	K	*Animal Waste 1993*
D	*Ceramic Sanitaryware 1978*	L	*White Salt 1986*
E	*Gas Appliances 1980*	M	*Concrete Roofing Tiles 1981*
F	*Ready Mixed Concrete 1981*	N	*Postal Franking Machines 1986*
G	*Tampons 1986*	O	*Tampons 1980*
H	*Soluble Coffee 1991*		

2 Historic costs basis.

3 For comparison, the average annual rate of return as obtained from a Bank of England analysis of the accounts of large companies varied between 14 and 18 per cent during the period 1978–87, and a later analysis gave average annual rates of return for manufacturing companies ranging from 13 to 21 per cent and averaging 17 per cent over the period 1989–92 (*Ice Cream 1994*).

7
Distribution, Licensing and Access

A   Introduction

Intervention by the regulatory authorities in the affairs of distributors and licensees has mainly been concerned with the *vertical restraints* that have been imposed on them by manufacturers and licensors. Regulatory practice in that respect came increasingly under question during the 1980s and 1990s, as a result of which the regimes now ruling differ substantially from those of the twentieth century. In its 1985 guidelines the US Department of Justice took the view that vertical restraints generally promote economic efficiency and it has since adopted a generally permissive attitude to them. A similar view was expressed by the British authorities during the passage into law of the Competition Act 1998, and the European authorities have since proposed a block exemption designed to avoid having to examine a wide range of beneficial or relatively harmless restrictions.

One consequence of this change of attitudes is that earlier cases now offer a limited guide to the likely treatment of particular business practices in this area. Taken in the context of recent official guidelines, they nevertheless retain a substantial degree of predictive value. Accordingly, this chapter deals first, in section B, with the general topic of the authorities' current attitudes to vertical restraints, before turning in section C to their earlier treatment of restraints upon distributors.

The constraints implied by the conditions attached to the licensing – or the refusal to license – of *patents*, *copyrights* and other intellectual property rights are restrictive agreements which are, in principle, subject to the prohibitions of Article 81[1] and of Chapter 1 of the Competition

---

[1] Article 81 of the Treaty of Amsterdam replaced Article 85 of the Treaty of Rome in 1997.

Act. The competition authorities have evolved a series of compromises between the avoidance of obstacles to competition and the need to promote innovation and creativity, and their attitudes to that dilemma are still developing. Section D below presents a guide to the current state of play. The European Commission and Courts also had to tackle the dilemmas presented by the conflict between the need to avoid barriers to trade between member states and the legitimate rights of owners of intellectual property rights and trade marks. Section D provides no more than a brief guide to the evolving situation, and readers should consult up-to-date legal texts for more detailed guidance.

The authorities' attitudes to the issues raised by the exercise of market power of distributors and of licensors are summarised in Sections E and F respectively and their treatment of questions relating to access to essential facilities is referred to in Section G.

All the technical terms employed are defined in Appendix 1.

B   Attitudes to vertical restraints

Following extensive consultation concerning the future treatment of vertical restraints, the European Commission stated[2] their objectives in dealing with vertical restraints to be the prevention of the following anti-competitive effects:

- the creation of obstacles to market integration;
- the foreclosure of markets to other suppliers or buyers;
- the deterioration of price- or non-price conditions available to consumers;
- the facilitation of collusion between suppliers.

The first of those objectives arises from Article 28[3] of the Treaty which requires that:

> Quantitative restrictions upon imports and all measures having equivalent effect shall ... be prohibited between Member States.

Among the qualifications[4] to Article 28 which appear in Article 30 are the statement that:

---

[2] Statement on Vertical Constraints OJ C365 26/11/98.

[3] Article 28 of the Treaty of Amsterdam replaced Article 30 of the Treaty of Rome in 1997.

[4] The other qualifications concern public morality, public policy or public security, health and so on.

The provisions of Articles 28 and 29 shall not preclude prohibitions or restrictions on imports, exports or goods in transit justified on grounds of... the protection of industrial and commercial property.

but that:

Such prohibitions or restrictions shall not, however, constitute a means of arbitrary discrimination or a diguised restriction on trade between Member States.

The Commission has been particularly eager to discourage restrictions upon *parallel imports*, which they regard as performing the valuable function of removing price discrimination between member states. Article 30 has, however, been important in its influence upon the ways in which the authorities have sought to resolve the conflicts between this objective and the preservation of intellectual property rights.

As regards the second of the above objectives, the Office of Fair Trading have noted that foreclosure of markets to suppliers might result from *exclusive buying or dealing* if potential retail outlets are tied to existing suppliers, and that *tie-in sales, full-line forcing and fidelity discounts* can have similar effects. Foreclosure of markets to retailers can result from exclusive distribution if widely practised by manufacturers: tie-in sales and full-line forcing can foreclose markets to those retailers who wish to specialise in a more limited product range; and quantity forcing can prevent entry by small-scale retailers. The possibility is accepted, however, that such detriments could be outweighed by efficiency gains resulting from *economies of scale or of scope* or from the avoidance of *free-rider* losses.[5]

The Office of Fair Trading has noted that the benefits of vertical restraints are more likely to outweigh anti-competitive effects in markets:

- for complex, technical, and relatively expensive products;
- for new products with weak branding;
- for one-off rather than repeat purchases;
- where customers have little knowledge of the product; and,
- where retailing involves few economies of scope between products of different manufacturers, and there are low barriers to entry.

[5] For example, under-investment because some of the benefits would go to free-riding competitors.

The last of the Commission's objectives is included in recognition of the possibility that vertical restraints could be used to preserve or augment market power, or to use market power at one level to create additional market power downstream – or possibly upstream – of that level. Because of that possibility (sometimes referred to as *leverage of market power*), the authorities have retained the power to prohibit those vertical restraints which can be deemed to be an abuse of a dominant position. At the same time they have relinquished some of their powers to regulate vertical restraints which are exercised in the absence of substantial market power.

In response to the comments received concerning proposals to amend the treatment of vertical restraints, the European Commission decided to replace the existing series of form-based block exemptions with a broader effects-based alternative[6] with a market-share threshold of 30 per cent. The *blacklisted* restraints which were to be excluded from that block exemption include resale price maintenance and absolute territorial protection. Exemptions from the requirement to notify agreements in order to obtain clearance under Article 81(3)[7] have been extended to apply to all vertical distribution agreements. The Commission noted when proposing the new block exemption that 'care has been taken to stay as close as possible to current policy as formulated in past Commission decisions and Court judgements'.

The treatment of vertical restraints remains subject to the long-established *ancillary restrictions* doctrine under which restrictions that are necessary for the success of a transaction that does not restrict competition cannot be considered to be anti-competitive. The European Court ruled that restrictions of that sort fall outside the prohibition of (what is now) Article 81(1), provided that they do not extend further in duration, scope or geographical application than is necessary to permit an agreement.[8]

Under the Competition Act 1998, provisions have been made for the exclusion of vertical agreements from the Chapter 1 prohibition. There is, however a claw-back provision enabling the Director-General to examine any agreement which he considers would infringe the prohibition and not merit an unconditional exemption. A Statutory Instrument excluding resale price maintenance from the exemption, and differing only in minor respects from the European Commission's block exemption, is under consideration.

[6] See p. 14.
[7] See p. 22.
[8] *Remia & Nutricia v. Commission* Case 42/84 [1985].

C   Restraints upon distributors

Resale price maintenance

The stipulation of fixed or minimum prices is expected to be prohibited under UK and European law, but there is no objection to the stipulation of maximum prices unless it is used to facilitate parallel pricing.

Franchising

Franchise agreements commonly restrict the franchisee's sources of supply and the geographical area in which he may operate. In return, the franchisor may undertake to limit the number of competing outlets to which franchises are granted.

In 1988, the European Commission published a block exemption[9] for franchise agreements (subsequently superseded by the vertical restraints block exemption). It exempted a wide range of specified restrictions, subject to a few conditions, including:

(a)   exclusion of reciprocal franchising agreements between competing suppliers;
(b)   the requirement that the franchisee should be free to set resale prices;
(c)   the requirement that the franchisee should be free to obtain supplies of the product from other franchisees or authorised dealers.
(d)   the requirement that the franchisee must reveal its status as an independent undertaking.

At that time, the Director-General of Fair Trading advised that geographic restrictions were generally unobjectionable under the Restrictive Trade Practices Act except when:

(a)   they are more than is reasonably necessary for the operation of the franchise; or,
(b)   the agreement disguises a market-sharing arrangement.

and that a restriction upon the franchisor not to compete in the territory of the franchisee was not likely to be prohibited if there is keen interbrand competition, nor was there likely to be any objection to a restriction upon the franchisee not to supply goods outside his territory. Recommended prices were not considered objectionable provided that the franchisee was free to charge lower prices.[10]

[9] Regulation 4087/88 of 30 November 1988.
[10] Howe 1988.

The Monopolies and Mergers Commission had earlier indicated[11] that no public interest issue was likely to arise from an obligation on a franchisee to obtain goods only from his franchisor, provided that:

(a)   the goods could be regarded as an essential part of the franchise package;
(b)   their precise nature and quality standards are important; and,
(c)   the goods could not readily and without disadvantage be obtained elsewhere.

Exclusive buying conditions had, for example, been considered to be justified in the case of mobile vans and ice-cream parlours, franchised for the sale of branded ice-cream, which were prominently identified by a supplier who provided support in terms of finance or of advice and training (*Ice Cream 1979*). On the other hand, the requirement that franchised car dealers should buy replacement parts only from the car manufacturer was considered to be against the public interest because the dealers could otherwise have obtained similar parts from independent component manufacturers (*Car Parts 1982*). However, the refusal of car manufacturers to supply parts except to their franchised dealers was later found not to be against the public interest, although it was considered to be a matter of 'potential concern' (*Car Parts 1992*).

Agency

Commercial agents, who negotiate or conclude transactions on behalf of principals, may under some circumstances escape regulation. In 1962, the European Commission advised that exclusive agencies of that type fall outside the prohibition of Article 81(1) of the Treaty and need not be notified, provided that the agent does not bear any of the risks of the transactions. Article 81(1) was, however, likely to apply if the agent:

(a)   maintains substantial stocks at his own expense;
(b)   provides a substantial free service to customers at his own expense; or,
(c)   is free to determine prices or terms of business.[12]

Article 81(1) had been held also to apply if the agent traded on his own account in the same commodity (*Suiker Unie 1976*), and possibly to apply if he acts for competing suppliers – even if he bears none of the risks arising from agency transactions.[13] Article 81(1) was not

---

[11]   *Full Line Forcing 1981.*
[12]   Commission Notice of 24 December 1962, JO 1962 2921.
[13]   Article 3 of Regulation 1983/83, referred to in section C below.

considered to apply to the appointment of an agent for a product in a given territory unless there is some restriction upon the action of the agent or his principal, or competition is otherwise affected. The Commission decided that the International Air Transport Association's (IATA) system of accredited marketing agents was subject to Article 81(1), even after unnecessary restrictions had been removed because little room remained for any other means of marketing air travel and freight. Exemption was granted under Article 81(3), however, after restrictions preventing IATA agents from working for non-IATA airlines (and vice versa) had been removed.

In 1981, the Monopolies and Mergers Commission noted that although the appointment of agencies restricts competition, the consumer would benefit from a better choice in the manufacturer's range and from better technical advice. The public interest was not, in its view, likely to be affected unless competition was unduly restricted.[14] The practice by a supplier of automotive components of forbidding its service agents – but not its other distributors – from buying competing components from other suppliers was considered not to be against the public interest because those agents were considered to be part of the supplier's distribution organisation (*Car Parts 1982*). The Commission did not fundamentally object to the selective and exclusive distribution system imposed by car manufacturers on dealers acting as factors, but sought the removal of some inessential restrictions (*Car Parts 1992*).

Restrictions arising from common ownership

In the European Union, the acquisition by a dominant supplier of a sufficient proportion of wholesale or retail outlets to enable it to restrict competition could be prohibited under Article 82 as an abuse of a dominant position, but there is no recorded case of such a prohibition. In the United Kingdom, the former Monopolies and Mergers Commission drew attention to dangers to the public interest if company-owned outlets were to provide a very high proportion of retail sales in any major retail market (*Petrol 1979*, par. 148). In that case it did not, however, regard company-ownership of 30 per cent of retail outlets for petrol, accounting for 50 per cent of retail sales, as being against the public interest – thereby reversing an earlier decision (*Petrol 1965*).

The ownership by brewers of 86 per cent of the public houses in England and Wales and their operation of the 'tied house system' were, however, found to operate against the public interest because they created entry

---

[14] *Full Line Forcing 1981.*

barriers and detriments to efficiency and to the interests of consumers (*Beer 1969*). The appropriate remedy was at that time considered to be reform of the licensing system. Following a subsequent inquiry, it was recommended on similar grounds that no brewer should be allowed to own or lease or have an interest in more than 2000 unlicensed outlets (*Beer 1989*). (A total ban on the ownership of licensed premises by brewers was rejected in order to protect those local brewers who are entirely dependent upon their tied estates because they do not have the resources to promote their brands nationally.) That recommendation was eventually rejected by the then Secretary of State, but the major brewers were ordered to relax some of the restrictions imposed upon their tenants in respect of half of the pubs owned by each brewer in excess of 2000. Instructions to subsidiaries which have the effect of protecting a national market against competition have also been prohibited (*Interbrew 1995*).[15]

Exclusive distribution

The regulatory authorities in the European Union have consistently condemned collective exclusive distribution agreements. Bilateral exclusive distribution agreements, on the other hand, have been held generally to lead to an improvement in distribution. Their use as a means of imposing resale price maintenance or of restricting exports or parallel imports has been prohibited.[16]

Bilateral exclusive distribution agreements concerning goods were otherwise exempt from Article 81(1) of the Treaty of Rome, subject to a number of conditions. To gain exemption they had to place no restriction upon the supplier other than an obligation not to supply the contract goods to others in the contract territory, and to place no obligations upon the distributor except:

(a) not to manufacture or distribute goods which compete with the contract goods;
(b) to obtain goods for resale only from the supplier;
(c) to refrain from seeking customers, or establishing branches or depots, outside the contract territory (but there must not be a ban on selling outside the contract territory);
(d) to purchase complete ranges or minimum quantities;
(e) to sell the contract goods under trademarks or packed and presented as specified by the supplier; or,
(f) to advertise promote and provide customer services for the product;

---

[15] Comp. Rep. 95, p. 140.
[16] *Junghans 1977, Zanussi 1978.*

nor could there be obstacles which made it difficult for purchasers to obtain the goods from outside the contract territory. Instructions to an exclusive distributor which obstructed parallel imports from within the EU attracted a heavy fine (*BASF/Accinauto 1995*).

The exemption did not apply where there were reciprocal exclusive dealing agreements between competing manufacturers nor where there was a non-reciprocal agreement involving a manufacturer with a turnover of more than 100 million ecu. It may be withdrawn by the Commission in particular cases.[17]

In negotiations with the Office of Fair Trading in 1984, the British Railways Board and the British Airports Authority agreed to abandon the practice of restricting those who may provide taxi or self-drive car-hire services at their stations and airports. The Director-General has indicated, however, that exclusive concessions of that type would not necessarily be considered to be anti-competitive if there were competition in the relevant market or if the concessions were awarded by competitive tendering at regular intervals.[18]

Selective distribution: qualitative criteria

Refusal to supply other than to retailers who meet criteria laid down by manufacturers has sometimes been approved by the competition authorities, even where price competition is thereby restricted. The European Court have confined approval to:

> high-quality and high-technology products which may justify a reduction of price competition in favour of competition relating to factors other than price.[19]

Approval has frequently been made conditional upon the removal of restrictions which the authorities have considered to be unnecessary. In the particular case of motor vehicles, there is automatic exemption from Article 81(1) for arrangements complying with Regulation 123/85 which permits a range of restrictions including restrictions upon sales of competitors' products. For other qualifying products, however, exemption of selective distribution agreements has not been given unless:

[17] Regulation 1983/83, OJ 1983 L173/1 & L281/24 and Commission Notice OJ 1984 C101/2.
[18] *British Airports Authority: Gatwick Airport 1984.*
[19] *AEG Telefunken 1983.*

(a)   they are based only upon objective criteria such as financial stability and the adequacy of staff and facilities;
(b)   those criteria are reasonably necessary to ensure an adequate distribution of the goods in question;
(c)   supply is not refused to anyone who meets those criteria nor permitted to anyone who does not; and,
(d)   the distributor is free to set his own prices and to deal in competing products.

The European Court had indicated, however, that should such a selective distribution system become so general as effectively to exclude other forms of distribution, the exemption would cease to apply (*Metro 1987*).

Other products requiring technically qualified retailers for which exemptions have been granted have included:

● cameras (*Kodak 1970*);
● personal computers (*IBM 1984*);
● watches (*Chanel 1995*);
● up-market perfumes and crystal glass – for which restrictions designed solely to preserve brand images have been exempted (*Yves Saint Laurent 1992, Givenchy 1992* and *Baccarat 1991*)

but a requirement that cosmetic products could be sold only by qualified practising pharmacists was considered to go beyond what was necessary to maintain the quality and proper use of the product (*Vichy 1991*).

The selective use of qualitative criteria by a dominant bicycle manufacturer in order to avoid supplying discount stores was investigated by the former Monopolies and Mergers Commission in 1981. The criteria included the provision of pre-delivery inspection and assembly, but that requirement was not applied consistently, as evidenced by the fact that 19 per cent of the manufacturer's bicycles were supplied to mail-order firms who did not offer those facilities. Although the Monopolies and Mergers Commission concluded that the practice was against the public interest, it effectively sanctioned its continuation by recommending only that the manufacturer should be required not to refuse supply to retailers who provide adequate pre-delivery inspection and assembly (*Bicycles 1981**). Refusal to supply power-tools to discounters was subsequently found to be against the public interest (*Black and Decker 1989**) but refusal to supply perfumes to the Superdrug retailer was approved on the grounds similar to those employed by the European Commission, namely that:

fine fragrances are marketed as luxury products and suppliers need to be able to control their distribution in order to protect the brand images which consumers evidently value.   (*Fine Fragrances 1993**)

A prohibition by a supplier of the renting of its video games was found to be against the public interest because it

deprives consumers of an important opportunity to experience games and make informed purchases.   (*Video Games 1995*)

Selective distribution: quantitative criteria

A somewhat different treatment was accorded to restrictions by suppliers upon the number of distributive outlets in a particular area. In an early case, the European Commission had exempted such an agreement concerning watches (*Omega 1970*), but subsequently the Commission stated that in such cases exemptions under Article 81(3) could be granted only in exceptional circumstances, and then only when the technical or other nature of the product is such that there must be close cooperation between manufacturer and dealer which could not be secured under some other system.[20] The block exemption for motor vehicles permitted such restrictions, but exemptions for other products had been rare.

In Britain, the practice had been considered to be justified under a range of circumstances. The Monopolies and Mergers Commission has noted that among the supplier's motives might be:

(a)   that to add to the number of outlets would increase his distribution costs without increasing his sales; or,

(b)   that he would do better by catering for a limited class of customer who is prepared to pay for exclusiveness.

The Commission saw no reason to treat refusal to supply for either of those reasons as being against the public interest when it is practised under reasonably competitive conditions.[21] In cases involving very limited competition among suppliers, the practice had been considered in several cases to be justified by its effects on distributors. It was considered to be in the public interest for the dominant wholesalers of newspapers to limit the number of retailers which they supplied and to select

[20] Comp. Report 5, 1976.
[21] *Refusal to Supply 1970.*

them on the basis of their location (*Newspapers 1978* and *1993*), and a similar practice was accepted in the bicycles case discussed above. Competition considerations were in those cases taken to be outweighed by the public interest in maintaining an effective distribution system, although the reports contained little by way of analysis of the consequences of relaxing the restrictions. The general argument that without restrictions on their numbers, retailers would lose profits and press for increased margins was accepted in one case (*Infant Milk Foods 1967*) but rejected in another (*Colour Film 1966*). In the latter case, the Commission thought that Kodak had been unnecessarily influenced by pressure from retailers and that the practice had served to keep their margins high.

Exclusive dealing

A similar but slightly less permissive treatment was generally accorded to a supplier's practice of requiring his distributors not to deal in his competitors' products (exclusive purchasing). The corresponding practice by a distributor of requiring his suppliers not to supply to other distributors (exclusive selling) seldom occurs outside exclusive distribution agreements – except in respect of distributors' own brands, for which it is considered to be harmless.[22] The conditions for exemption of exclusive purchasing agreements from the prohibition of Article 81(1) are similar – with the exception of references to a contract area – to those for exclusive distribution agreements which have been listed above. The exemption did not, however, apply if the agreement was for an indefinite duration or for a period of more than five years – with exceptions in that and other respects for sellers of beer and petrol.[23] Certain restrictions occurring under agency and franchise agreements were also exempt.

Exclusive purchasing conditions were, however, prohibited if they foreclosed a substantial part of a market (*Hoffman-La Roche 1979, Mars 1992*) or if they restricted the ability of competitors to increase their market share (*Delimitis v. Bräu 1992*), and the same applied to loyalty rebates which tend to have the same effect (*Suiker Unie 1976*). The offer of favourable delivery times to exclusive stockists in time of shortage had also been considered by the Commission to be an abuse of a dominant position (*British Gypsum 1988*). Agreements under which an aircraft manufacturer gave discounts to airlines that undertook not to

---

[22] *Refusal to Supply 1970.*
[23] Regulation 1984/83.

buy from its competitors had to be abandoned as a condition for the authorisation of a merger (*Boeing/McDonnell Douglas 1997*).

In the UK the practice had in some cases been voluntarily abandoned following an informal investigation under the Competition Act 1980 (for example, Kango Wolf in OFT guide) or after a formal investigation had found it to be anti-competitive (*Petter 1981*). The provision of large discounts to its own agents by a supplier of catering equipment was also stopped after it had been found to be anti-competitive (*Still 1982*). A condition imposed by a locally dominant newspaper that prevented newsagents from also handling free-sheet papers was found to be anti-competitive and was referred to the Monopolies and Mergers Commission. The Commission found the practice to be against the public interest but considered that the newspaper was entitled to protect itself against a selective attack by free-sheets which was aimed exclusively at its own readership (*Sheffield Newspapers 1982*). Restrictions imposed by Coca Cola on the sales of competing products, revealed in the course of a monopoly investigation, were, however, deemed to be against the public interest (*Carbonated Drinks 1991*).

The Monopolies and Mergers Commission had been prepared to accept that exclusive buying could, in some circumstances, enhance competition. It was considered that competition in the promotion of a brand image and in the provision of spares and servicing might be keener when each distributor is committed to one supplier's products. Prices were in any case thought likely to be nearly uniform when the product is a homogeneous commodity (*Liquefied Petroleum Gas 1981*).

An exclusive buying agreement with an agent or a franchisee had been considered acceptable under some circumstances, but the practice was found to be against the public interest in a case in which it prevented franchised dealers from obtaining competing products which were readily available from other sources (*Car Parts 1982*).

It was noted in that case that the offer of discounts which are conditional upon maintaining a particular volume of sales or of stocks can have the effect of exclusive dealing, and in another case the abandonment of such practices and of unnecessarily long-term contracts was recommended (*Metal Containers 1970*). Loyalty rebates could have a similar effect, but might be justifiable by cost savings. In a case in which the product was made to the customer's specification and loyalty rebates were not strictly related to cost savings, the practice was nevertheless considered to be justified as a means of obtaining savings from long production runs (*Flat Glass 1968*). The same effect often resulted from the provision at nominal rental of refrigerated cabinets for ice-cream on the condition that they were used only for the supplier's products. That practice was, however, considered justifiable because sales might otherwise fall and competition and consumer choice might be reduced (*Ice Cream 1979* and *1994*).

Full-line forcing and tie-in sales

Under some circumstances, the competition authorities have sought to regulate the practice under which it is made a condition of supply that the purchaser buys the full range of a particular class of products (full-line forcing), and the practice under which it is made a condition that he also buys certain other products (tie-in sales). Their main concern was to prevent the use of market power over one product to acquire market power over another. The practices were consequently likely to escape regulation except when they were used by dominant firms for that purpose.

Articles 81(1) and 82 of the Treaty of Amsterdam both prohibit the practice of:

> making the conclusion of contracts subject to acceptance by other parties of supplementary obligations which, by their nature or according to commercial usage, have no connection with such contracts.

Full-line forcing may be expected to escape the prohibition of Article 81(1) if it is part of a franchise, exclusive distribution or purchasing agreement which meets the requirements of the regulations referred to above. The practices which are specifically permitted under those regulations did not include tie-in sales, but that practice appears also to have escaped condemnation by the Commission under Article 81(1). The practices thus appeared likely to be prohibited and to attract penalties only if they were employed by organisations occupying dominant positions under the terms of Article 82.[24] Tying arrangements between brewers and their outlets were covered by the rules of Regulation No. 1984/3.

Among the practices at issue in the informal negotiations which led to the 1984 settlement between the Commission and IBM[25] were IBM's refusal to sell the memory units of one of their computers separately from its central processing unit and not offering the system without the

---

[24] See p. 69.
[25] See Competition Report 14 1985 and *Competition Newsletter* 1998 No 3.

basic software. Under less complex circumstances, the Commission have also objected to the tying together of hardware and software services by a dominant supplier (*Digital 1997*) but in the absence of dominance, the tying of printer consumables was considered acceptable (*Pelikan/Kyocera 1995*). Europe's largest manufacturer of power-tools was fined for abuse of a dominant position in that they tied the supply of nails to the supply of cartridges (*Hilti 1988*) and a major supplier of packaging machines was fined for tying the use of their cartons to the use of their machines (*Tetra Pak 1991*).

The possibility of prohibiting full-line forcing and tie-in sales was considered by an interdepartmental committee in 1979[26] as a result of which a general reference was made to the Monopolies and Mergers Commission under Section 83 of the Fair Trading Act. For the purpose of that reference, the practices were taken to include:

> making the supply of goods or services available at prices or upon terms as to credit, discount or otherwise which are so disadvantageous as to be likely to deter that person or class of persons from acquiring those goods or services without acquiring other goods or services.

The Commission concluded that the practices are not always against the public interest, and that existing powers under the Fair Trading Act and the Competition Act were adequate for its regulation.[27] The practices were considered to be justified under franchise agreements under the circumstances described in section B above. In their report, the Commission noted that 'where a supplier has substantial market power... the exclusionary effect on competitors is likely to be against the public interest' but that 'If a tie forecloses only a small part of the market and there are numerous other outlets available the effect... may be negligible.' No objection was raised against the practice by a company with a 60 per cent market share of offering discounts conditional upon the stocking of the full range of their products (*Tambrands 1996*).

The distinction between justifiable and unjustifiable uses of tie-in sales had been illustrated by a case in which the rental terms for copying machines which had been imposed by a dominant supplier had included spares and servicing and the supply of a chemical referred to as 'toner'. The Commission found the control of spares and servicing to

---

[26] DTI 1979.
[27] *Full Line Forcing 1981.*

be justified by the need to protect the performance of the machines, but found that the policy regarding toner was against the public interest (*Reprographic Equipment 1976*). But that restriction was not considered objectionable some 14 years later, by which time the market share of the supplier had dropped from 90 per cent to 31 per cent (*Photocopiers 1991*). The supply of colour film only at prices which included a charge for processing had also been found to be against the public interest (*Colour Film 1966*) as was the tying of the sale of soft ice-cream to the sale of hard ice-cream (*Ice Cream 1979*). The Commission condemned an arrangement under which a hirer of an exhibition hall was compelled to employ only listed electricians (*Exhibition Halls 1990*). But it was considered to be an acceptable business practice to use the proceeds from the sales of caravans to subsidise the rentals of caravan sites and to reserve sites – 70 per cent of which were controlled by the caravan sellers in question – for buyers of their caravans (*Caravan Sites 1983*).

D Licensing agreements

Technology transfer

The European Commission's treatment of patents and know-how agreements is governed by the terms of the block exemption for technology transfer,[28] which replaced two separate block exemptions in 1996. The following restrictions are exempted from the prohibition of Article 81(1):

an obligation on the licensor

- not to license other undertakings to exploit the licensed technology in the licensed territory;
- not to exploit the licensed technology in the licensed territory himself;

an obligation on the licensee

- not to exploit the licensed technology in the territory of the licensor within the common market;
- not to manufacture or use the licensed product, or use the licensed process, in territories within the common market which are licensed to other licensees;
- not to pursue an active policy of putting the licensed product on the market in the territories within the common market which

[28] Regulation 240/96.

are licensed to other licensees, and in particular not to engage in advertising specifically aimed at those territories or to establish any branch or maintain any distribution depot there;

- not to put the licensed product on the market in the territories licensed to other licensees within the common market in response to unsolicited orders;
- to use only the licensor's trademark or get up to distinguish the licensed product during the term of the agreement, provided that the licensee is not prevented from identifying himself as the manufacturer of the licensed products;
- to limit his production of the licensed product to the quantities he requires in manufacturing his own products and to sell the licensed product only as an integral part of or a replacement part for his own products or otherwise in connection with the sale of his own products provided that such quantities are freely determined by the licensee.

That list is supplemented by a more detailed 'white list' of restrictions which are deemed rarely to infringe the prohibition and which are also exempted. There is also a 'black list' of restrictions which would prevent the exemption of an agreement, the principal of which are those in which one party is restricted in the determination of prices for the licensed product or is restricted from competing within the common market with the other party.

It is not certain how far the attitudes reflected in these rules can be read across to design rights, copyrights and trade marks. Software licences are given separate protection.[29]

The withholding of licences

The unreasonable refusal to grant licences may on its own be considered to be a strengthening or an abuse of a dominant position. The acquisition of the results of government-funded R&D in consequence of a proposed merger was held to contribute to strengthening Boeing's dominant position, and an undertaking was obtained from Boeing to grant non-exclusive licences for patents and know-how (*Boeing/MDD 1997*). The refusal by television stations to allow the publication of details of television programmes on which they held copyrights was condemned because its motive was to exclude competition from the market for television guides (*Television Guides 1988 and*

[29] Council Directive 91/250 on the legal protection of computer programs OJ L122/42 1991g.

1991). The refusal of a British car manufacturer to grant licences other than to its own suppliers for the manufacture of replacement body parts was found by the Monopolies and Mergers Commission to be against the public interest because it raised the prices of spares, and because motorists would be compelled to scrap older cars if the spares ceased to be available (*Ford 1985*), and the European Commission obtained an undertaking from the company to offer the necessary licences. The European Court subsequently ruled that the exercise of an exclusive right could be prohibited under Article 82 if it involved:

> the arbitrary refusal to supply spare parts to independent repairers, the fixing of prices for spare parts at an unreasonable level, or a decision no longer to produce spare parts for a particular model....
> (*Volvo 1999*)

An exclusive licence was ruled to be an abuse of a dominant position because it deprived a competitor of the use of new technology (*Tetra Pak 1988 and 1990*) even though, as an agreement, it fell within the terms of a block exemption.

Restrictions on the movement of goods

The European Commission has long been concerned to limit the use of intellectual property rights to restrict the movement of goods across national boundaries within the common market. A very large number of EU cases were for a time concerned with that problem.[30] The precedents established by those cases are complex, but some straightforward rules can be distinguished. Under a principle known as *exhaustion of rights*, it has been established that a national patent may not be used to prevent imports of a product which the owner of the patent has previously marketed in another member state (*Deutsche Grammophon 1971, Merck v Stephar 1981*). On the other hand a patentee is entitled to exercise patent rights to prevent the import of products sold by a third party in another country where no patent protection is available (*Parke Davis 1968*). Harmonising regulations[31] have since been introduced in order to prevent restrictions arising from differences between national intellectual property laws within the community.

[30] Summaries of 26 such cases appear in Bellamy and Child 1987, Chapter 7.
[31] Council Directive 93/98/EEC on copyrights and Council Regulation 40/94 on trade marks.

The European authorities have applied a variety of legal interpretations to Article 30 to limit its use in preventing parallel imports *within* the community, but the Court has controversially supported the use of a trade mark to prohibit parallel imports from outside the European Economic Area. In 1998, the Court ruled that imports of branded goods from outside the EEA without the consent of the brand owner violated EU trademark rules (*Silhouette 1998*).

E   The market power of retailers

The regulatory authorities in Britain and elsewhere in the Community have exhibited some concern about the growth of concentration in some retailing areas, particularly in food retailing by supermarkets.

The supermarkets

In Britain, three large firms now account for over 50 per cent of supermarket grocery sales. The Monopolies and Mergers Commission has drawn attention to fears that a handful of large multiples might come to dominate the distributive trades, to the disadvantage of suppliers and consumers,[32] and the Government have indicated that any proposed acquisitions by those large multiples should be referred to the Commission.[33] However, the mergers which have occurred have usually involved only the smaller supermarket chains, and have escaped reference on the ground that they would serve to strengthen their ability to complete with the large chains. No evidence of abuse of distributors' market power has yet emerged, the indications being that they use that power mainly to buy produce at reduced prices, and that most of the savings are passed on to consumers. A subsequent investigation commissioned by the Office of Fair Trading noted that trends in concentration and average gross and net margins had since increased, which the authors took to suggest that retailers are increasingly able to retain benefits from their increased bargaining power rather than passing them to consumers.[34] After a subsequent investigation by the Office of Fair Trading, the Director-General expressed concern about barriers to entry and about a tendency to set prices to match the competition rather than undercut them, and announced that he had referred the matter to the Competition Commission.[35]

[32] *Discounts to Retailers 1981.*
[33] Hansard, 27 January 1988.
[34] Dobson, Waterson and Chu 1998.
[35] Press release PN 11/99 of 8 April 1999.

Joint buying

In France and West Germany, there has been concern that the practice among small retailers of forming 'buying groups' in order to obtain discounts from their suppliers, has recently spread to the larger retailing chains, with the formation of 'super buying groups'. However, inquiries by the regulatory authorities have generally led to the conclusion that the market power of the larger groups has not yet reached such a level as to warrant intervention.

Concern by the European Commission has led to the commissioning of a special study of the effects of concentration in retailing, but the authors then concluded that the buying power of distributors had not generally been abused.[36] The European Court has ruled that joint buying associations which impose no exclusive buying obligations on their members will not normally be held to infringe Article 81(1) of the Treaty,[37] and the Commission has indicated that it would in any case be willing to grant exemptions where the agreement enables retailers to obtain fair terms and does not put undue pressure on suppliers. The Commission has given approval to an European Economic Interest Grouping (EEIG) of seven medium-sized pharmaceutical wholesalers, which incorporated a buying agreement under which members remained free to determine prices and conditions of sale of their products (*EEIG Orphe 1990*).

In the United Kingdom, the Office of Fair Trading issued the following guidance concerning the circumstances under which it would seek an order not to proceed against a joint buying agreement in the former Restrictive Practices Court:

> A number of agreements for group buying include recommendations for the price to be charged for goods covered by special promotions of 'own brand' goods. Such recommendations are likely to be registrable restrictions but may not be considered significantly anti-competitive if members are free to charge lower prices if they wish and, in the case of promotions, provided that those are for a short time and the recommended price is lower than that usually charged.

Some restrictions in group buying agreements have had to be modified or abandoned before representations could be made. These include:

– allocation of geographical areas to particular members;

[36] Competition Report 16 1987, p. 236.
[37] *Spar 1975*.

- wholesalers not to supply or sponsor retailers outside defined areas;
- wholesalers or retailers to purchase minimum quantities through the group;
- members not to join any other group.[38]

F   The abuse of intellectual property rights

The treatment of refusals to grant licences is dealt with in section D above. The amassing of patents by a dominant supplier has also been regarded as an abuse. The Xerox Group had over a thousand patents and patent applications pertaining to photocopying, had been unwilling to grant licences, and had opposed the granting of patents to others. Those practices were found to be against the public interest because they had compelled potential competitors to spend a lot of time and money finding the extent of Xerox's patent protection and developing alternatives which were often inferior (*Reprographic Equipment 1976*). The availability of alternatives may, however, be decisive. The ownership by Kodak of ten patents which were of major importance in the manufacture and processing of colour film was held not to constitute an entry barrier because its competitors had been able to develop comparable products by other methods (*Colour Film 1966*).

The withholding of interface information by a dominant firm, for the purpose of creating market power over connected equipment, has also been condemned. In 1980, the European Commission alleged that IBM had infringed Article 82 by failing to supply other manufacturers the technical information needed to permit competitive products to be used with its System 370. Undertakings[39] were obtained from IBM that subsequently had a major effect upon the computer industry.

Horizontal licensing agreements by dominant firms are almost certain to be regarded as infringements of Article 82 or Chapter II of the Competition Act. The European Commission has several times taken action against patent pools.[40] Action against cross-licensing was considered on one occasion by the Monopolies and Mergers Commission. A manufacturer had agreed to give its dominant competitor the option to obtain non-exclusive licences for up to eight of its patents. The Commission thought it arguable that such an agreement was anti-competitive because it gave the dominant firm the right to take advantage of any technological breakthrough by its main rival, and thus helped to

---

[38] OFT guides: *Restrictive Practices*.
[39] See Competition Policy *Newsletter* 1998, No. 3, p. 7.
[40] See for example, Competition Report No. 11, 1981, p. 62.

preserve its dominant position. Prohibition of the agreement was not recommended because of its non-exclusive nature, and because of the danger of rendering the dominant British firm more vulnerable to overseas competition (*Postal Franking Machines 1986*). Restrictions upon the application of UNIX to the version developed by Microsoft were removed under pressure from the Commission (*Microsoft/Santa Cruz 1997*).

G   Access to essential facilities

The European Commission have been developing their approach to the refusal of access to facilities which are necessary for the conduct of commercial activities. That approach has been developed principally in connection with ports, but it is likely to have wider application to public utilities, including airports, railways and communications[41] and distribution networks.

An *essential facility* is deemed to be one to which access is essential to entry into a market, for which alternatives are not available and cannot be created without great difficulty. Refusal to supply is effectively prohibited unless it can be shown to be done for a commercial reason other than the obstruction of competition.

The Office of Fair Trading has noted that:

> It is questionable whether the owner of an essential facility should be obliged to give up capacity to accommodate new entrants where there are capacity constraints.... An important consideration will be whether facilitating new entry... will lead to an increase in competition.... Pricing behaviour and previous refusal of access may be taken into account.... In some instances, there may be an obligation on the facility owner to create more capacity if it is feasible to do so.[42] Where there is spare capacity... refusal to grant access... is likely to constitute an abuse.

---

[41] Public communications operators are required under the EC Open Network Provision to provide open and efficient access to their networks.

[42] For instance, the licence and statutory obligations on UK public utilities.

Part III
The Impact of Competition Policy

8
Trends: the Past and the Present

A Introduction

The review of the conduct of competition policy in Part II has been mainly concerned with the authorities' treatment of business practices in the course of the last 20 to 30 years. Competition policy has been presented in static terms – as though it had sprung into existence, fully developed, in the course of the 1970s. In fact, the conduct of competition policy has developed over a period of over 50 years, and it is still developing. A review of the impact of policy must therefore take account of earlier developments and of current trends.

Changes in the conduct of competition policy have occurred for a number of reasons. Its intellectual framework has been refined over the years, and there have been analytical innovations, some of which – such as the theory of contestable markets – remain a matter of controversy. Attitudes and beliefs – concerning, for example, freedom of contract and the advantages of size – have undergone radical change. Administrative institutions and procedures have evolved, sometimes haphazardly, and have adapted to the tasks and resource limitations which have faced them. Arbitrary criteria have been established to define jurisdiction and to distinguish between abusive and acceptable practices. Precedents have been established and overturned, and the predictability of the attitudes of the regulatory authorities to many business practices has increased.

The process of development has not, however, reached a stage at which further change is likely to be confined to relatively minor adjustments. There remain substantial areas of business behaviour the regulatory treatment of which is still evolving, and on which evidence is incomplete or methods of analysis have yet to be established. The effectiveness and efficiency of existing methods of regulation are being questioned, and major institutional and procedural changes are under consideration.

As a background to the consideration in the concluding chapter of likely future developments, this chapter reviews the past development of competition policy, considers its direct impact on the behaviour and structure of some of the industries with which it has been concerned and examines the extent of its indirect influence upon others.

B   The development of policy

United Kingdom policy

The common law origins

Textbooks on British competition law trace its origins to the thirteenth century in the development of the common law doctrine of restraint of trade.[1] Although that doctrine was founded upon the idea that there were public policy consequences of restraints upon trade, the interpretations put upon it in the late nineteenth century were concerned solely with reasonableness between the parties to an agreement. It was generally held that an agreement that was unreasonably in restraint of trade was unenforceable as between the parties to that agreement, but that third parties had no legitimate interest in the matter. Later decisions modified that interpretation, but at the time, it seemed that the doctrine had ceased to have any relevance for competition policy.

The apparent collapse of the doctrine of the restraint of trade as an instrument of competition policy led in the United States to the passing of the Sherman Act,[2] but no British legislation on the subject was introduced until 1948. In the years following the First World War, policy action was discouraged by the belief that cartels and 'rationalisation' would be a means of preserving British industry in the face of the overcapacity which had been brought about by a collapse in demand, and of competition from large firms overseas. The reluctance to legislate on the matter was reinforced – or rationalised – by an appeal to the principle of freedom of contract. For example, the Committee on Restraint of Trade reported in 1930 that:

> We hold that the ordinary right of freedom of contract ought not to be withdrawn without some compelling reason. We do not regard the price maintenance system as free from disadvantages from the public

[1] See, for example, Whish 1993.
[2] See p. 16.

point of view, but we are not satisfied that if a change in the law were made there is any reason to think that the interests of the public would be better served.[3]

Postwar legislation

By 1944, however, the – by then extensive – cartelisation of British industry was being seen as an impediment to postwar reconstruction, and a government White Paper[4] on employment proposed the creation of powers for the government to:

> inform themselves of the extent and effect of restrictive agreements and the activities of combines; and to take appropriate action to check practices which may bring advantages to the sectional producing interests, but work to the detriment of the country as a whole.

The Monopolies and Restrictive Practices (Inquiry and Control) Act 1948 set up the Monopolies and Restrictive Practices Commission, to inquire on request into the effects upon the public interest of the activities of individual firms or combinations of firms which supplied 30 per cent or more of any market for goods. The Act did not specify any public interest criterion and did not mention competition. It gave powers to the (then) Board of Trade to make references and to apply remedies in response to adverse public-interest findings. Early inquiries revealed the abuse of market power by monopolies, such as the excessive profits of the Anglo-Swedish match monopoly, and extensive cartelisation, among, for example, the suppliers of electric lamps and of cables. In nearly all of the 20 cases investigated by the Commission between 1948 and 1956, practices were revealed which were found to be against the public interest.

Restrictive practices

In 1952, the Board of Trade called for a general inquiry into collective discrimination (exclusive dealing, collective boycotts, and the like) and the Commission's majority report on the subject recommended in 1955 that the collective imposition of such restrictions should be made a criminal offence, subject to exceptions to be adjudicated by an independent body.[5] The government accepted instead the minority

---

[3] Quoted in *Collective Discrimination 1955*, Appendix 1.
[4] Cmnd 6527.
[5] *Collective Discrimination 1955*.

recommendation for the registration of agreements, followed by prohibition of all except those which were found not to be against the public interest. The Restrictive Trade Practices Act 1956 contained provisions similar to those of the later (1976) legislation, except that it excluded information agreements and agreements relating to the supply of services, and that unregistered agreements were not made legally void.

The legislation had a dramatic impact. Following the second case brought before the Restrictive Practices Court in 1959, most parties to registrable agreements concluded that there was little prospect that the Court would allow them to continue, and that there was no point in incurring the great expense of attempting to defend them. Analysis of registrations indicated that some 50 to 60 per cent of UK manufacturing output had been subject to cartel restrictions[6] but in the following ten years over 30 000 agreements were abandoned – only 39 of them as a result of judgements by the Court. There is evidence to suggest, however, that a substantial number of agreements – possibly 13 per cent of those existing before 1956 – continued to be operated in secret.[7]

Collectively enforced resale price maintenance was effectively eliminated by the 1956 Act, but individually enforced resale price maintenance was not brought under control until the passing of the Resale Prices Act 1964, under which it was prohibited unless exempted by order of the Court. Again, the impact was dramatic. Resale price maintenance is estimated to have applied to 20 to 25 per cent of consumers' expenditure in 1960, and by 1979 it applied only to books and medicines – covering less than 2 per cent of consumers' expenditure.

The restrictive practices legislation applied initially only to the suppliers of goods, but it was extended in 1976 to include the suppliers of services. There were exceptions, however, including agricultural marketing boards, transport operators, and virtually all professional services. In 1967, the Monopolies and Mergers Commission was asked to make a general inquiry into restrictions upon entry, upon the charging of fees, upon advertising, and upon other restrictive practices in the professions. The Commission concluded that the practices revealed by its inquiries were likely to be against the public interest.[8]

There followed a series of references to the Commission and negotiations by the Office of Fair Trading, resulting in the relaxation of restrictions on scale fees and advertising imposed by professional bodies on architects and surveyors, solicitors, accountants, stockbrokers, opticians

[6] Elliott and Gribbin 1977.
[7] Swann *et al.* 1974.
[8] *Professional Services 1970.*

and veterinary surgeons. A further review undertaken by the Office of Fair Trading in 1986 led to negotiations with professional associations concerning restrictions upon working with members of other professions in mixed practices.

An interdepartmental committee set up to review the legislation reported in 1988 that it was

> inflexible and slow, too often concerned with cases which are obviously harmless and not directed sufficiently at anti-competitive agreements. The scope for avoidance and evasion considerably weakens any deterrent effect the system has and enforcement powers are inadequate. The requirement to furnish insignificant agreements is not only wasteful of official resources but it imposes an excessive burden on firms.[9]

On the advice of the committee, the government announced its intention to introduce an effects-based system along the lines of Article 81. It was not until ten years – and one administration – later that the Competition Act 1998 put that intention into effect, repealing the Restrictive Trade Practices Act and introducing a prohibition, procedures and penalties which were closely modelled on Article 81 of the Treaty of Amsterdam.

Mergers

The prewar belief that the concentration of firms into larger units would increase their efficiency continued to be held by many industrialists and politicians well into the 1960s. Merger activity in the mid-1960s was at over five times its 1950 level, and was making a major contribution to the growth in concentration in manufacturing industry. In 1966, the government set up the Industrial Reorganisation Corporation for the purpose of encouraging selected mergers. By that time, however, there was also a recognition that mergers could in some circumstances be harmful. The Monopolies and Mergers Act 1965 was framed on the assumption that although mergers were on the whole beneficial, a selected few should be investigated, and that those which could be shown to be damaging to the public interest should be prohibited.

In the early 1970s, evidence was mounting which showed that the expected efficiency gains from mergers had not materialised, and there was a change in the climate of opinion. In 1971, the Industrial

[9] DTI 1988.

Reorganisation Corporation was disbanded. The policy presumption in favour of mergers was challenged in 1978 by an interdepartmental committee which recommended that policy should be shifted to a neutral position.[10] In the following years, however, the belief that most mergers are beneficial in themselves gave way to a belief that the merger process contributes to economic efficiency by establishing a 'market for corporate control'.[11] The proposed policy change was rejected, and the policy presumption in favour of mergers remains substantially as it was in the 1960s. There have since been a number of changes designed to speed up the mergers procedures and reduce their burden on firms, apart from which, regulatory procedures also remain as they were in the 1960s

The abuse of market power

In respect of defined monopoly situations, the Fair Trading Act 1973 gave the Commission unlimited power to recommend remedies. It gave the Secretary of State unlimited powers to implement those or other remedies, but in respect only of matters which the Commission had found to be against the public interest. The remedies which the Commission recommended almost invariably involved the cessation of anticompetitive practices rather than the reduction of market power by the divestment of subsidiaries. The single exception was the gas monopoly, the divestment of whose trading activities was recommended[12] but not, at that time, implemented. The Director-General was given few investigative powers, and no formal powers to make public-interest judgements or initiate remedies although in practice he acquired considerable powers in those respects from his function of negotiating undertakings. The scope for seeking undertakings in lieu of references was extended by the Deregulation and Contracting Out Act 1994 and the Director-General's powers in those respects were correspondingly enhanced.

In an attempt to provide for an effective but less cumbersome means of inquiry than was provided for by the Restrictive Practices and Fair Trading Acts, the Competition Act 1980 introduced a two-stage procedure under which the Director-General could undertake a formal inquiry into any anti-competitive practice by a qualifying firm and then decide whether to refer it to the Commission. The Deregulation Act 1994 removed the former of those stages of formal investigation but

[10] DTI 1978.
[11] See p. 77.
[12] *Gas 1993*.

left the Director-General with the powers of investigation which the Competition Act had provided for that stage. Comparatively little formal use has been made of those powers, but they were widely used informally by the Director-General to persuade firms to abandon practices that he considered to be anti-competitive.

Section 11 of the Competition Act 1980 also provided for inquiries by the Commission into the efficiency of public-sector organisations,[13] and an extensive programme of such inquiries followed in the course of the 1980s. As the government's privatisation programme proceeded, regulation of the public utilities affected was assigned to government-appointed regulators, leaving the Commission with the role of determining appeals against their decisions. The Director-General's powers in regard to anti-competitive practices were not formally altered, but in practice his office subsequently exercised a growing degree of cooperation with the regulators.

In 1992 in a consultative document, the Government noted that existing legislation provided a relatively weak deterrent against the abuse of market power and put forward three options, one of which would be a legal prohibition along the lines of Article 82 of the Treaty of Amsterdam.[14] The government of the day announced that it had chosen instead the option of strengthening existing legislation by giving greater powers to the Director-General and introducing liability for civil damages – although it acknowledged that this would not fully address the issue of weak deterrence.[15] That decision was not put into effect, however, and the next administration introduced an Article 82-type prohibition in the Competition Act 1998. Much of the Fair Trading Act 1973 was repealed by that Act, but powers to refer a monopoly to the Competition Commission were retained and held in reserve. A number of administrative changes were introduced in the late 1990s to increase the transparency of the work of the competition authorities.

European Union Policy

Origins

The first measure of competition policy adopted on a European basis was incorporated in the Treaty of Paris, which set up the European Coal and Steel Community. This gave jurisdiction to a 'High Authority' to deal with restraints on competition within member states, whether or

[13] As described on p. 29.
[14] DTI 1992.
[15] DTI press notice of 14/4/93.

not they affected trade between member states. The Coal and Steel Community came into operation in 1953. Discussions among the six members of that community led to the signing of the Treaty of Rome, which came into effect in 1958. The formulation in that treaty of an effects-based system which made prohibited practices void unless exempted by the competition authority, owed a great deal to the outcome of the debate in West Germany which had led to the passing there of the Act Against Restraints of Competition (1957).

Restrictive practices and the abuse of a dominant position

Community competition policy did not, however, come fully into operation until after the ratification in 1962 of Regulation 17, governing regulatory procedures, including the procedures for notification and exemption.[16] In the following two years, the European Commission was fully engaged in processing upwards of 35 000 notifications, and its first formal decision was not issued until 1964. Substantial powers had been delegated to the Commission by the Council of the European Communities and in 1964 and the following few years, a firm legal foundation for its policies was established by the – mainly supportive – decisions of the European Court of Justice. The burden of dealing with notifications under Regulation 17 continued to dominate the Commission's activities for many years, however, and priority had to be given to the resolution of concerted practices under the then Article 85, particularly those relating to distribution and patent licensing. Action against the numerous cartels known to be operating in the Community was thus postponed, and it was not until 1969 that the Commission imposed fines upon a cartel. Action against abuse of a dominant position was similarly delayed, and the Commission's first formal decision under Article 86 was not taken until 1971.

The Commission's overload has since been substantially reduced by the introduction of regulations based upon established case law which have granted group exemptions to a range of agreements and practices and have thus reduced the need for notifications and case-by-case clearances. Simplified procedures including informal negotiations with firms and the issue of 'comfort letters' have also helped to reduce the Commission's backlog of notifications and complaints. Time became available to tackle horizontal restrictions and action was taken against cartels affecting quinine, dyestuffs, zinc, aluminium, parchment, glass, woodpulp and polypropylene and others. Article 85 cases continued to predominate,

---

[16] Described on p. 39.

but some of the relatively few Article 86 cases – involving abuse of a dominant position – may have had more far-reaching consequences.

After extensive consultation following the publication in 1997 of a Green Paper on the subject, the Commission proposed a new regulation exempting most categories of vertical restraint for firms with market shares less than 30 per cent. A review of policy toward horizontal agreements is to follow. In April 1999, the European Commission published a White Paper proposing the abolition of the notification and exemption system.

State aids and restrictions on public utilities

Since the mid-1970s the Commission has also mounted a progressively more determined attack upon state aids and other anticompetitive practices by the governments of member states. In the five years from 1977 to 1981 3 per cent of the 628 state aids examined by the Commission were ruled against or withdrawn; in the subsequent five years the percentage rose to 8 per cent of 1132 cases. Concealed subsidies in privatisation measures have been restrained, as in the case of the sale of the Rover Group to British Aerospace in 1988. State aids to agriculture are, however, exempt from regulation, except for products receiving Community support under the Common Agricultural Policy. Regulations concerning land transport and sea transport were introduced in 1968 and 1986, and in 1987 a regulation was issued which limited price-fixing in air transport, followed in 1989 by a ruling by the European Court of Justice enabling the Commission to prohibit price-fixing agreements applying to flights between member countries.

Mergers

Following a decision by the European Court that Article 86 could under some circumstances be used to regulate mergers, the Commission prepared a draft regulation in 1973 which would have given them wider and better-defined powers. In response to opposition from Britain and other member states, further drafts were put forward in 1982, 1984, 1986, 1988 and the terms of a regulation were finally agreed in December 1989. However, the Commission were then already able to exert a substantial degree of informal influence over large cross-border merger proposals, and a number of mergers which had been cleared by national authorities had been re-examined and modified. The turnover thresholds above which the European Commission were given jurisdiction were higher than the Commission had wanted, but were made subject to review by the end of 1993. After extensive consultation involving the business community, legal practitioners and the member states, the Commission then concluded that, although there were strong arguments for lower thresholds, more experience should be gained before making any formal changes to the regulation. The reduction was finally agreed and the current thresholds were introduced in 1997.

International cooperation

The European Commission claim jurisdiction over any agreement or practice that has a prohibited effect within the European Union, even if the companies concerned are located outside the union and do not operate within it. The competition authorities in the United States take a similar view. The Organisation for Economic Cooperation and Development has developed a range of proposals for avoiding or resolving the consequent conflicts of jurisdiction, the latest of which was published in 1995.[17] In 1998, the OECD issued further proposals under the title of *Recommendation on Hard Core Cartels*.

A bilateral EU/US agreement came into force in 1991 and its cooperation procedures were effective in regulating the mergers between Boeing and McDonnell-Douglas in 1997 and between WorldCom and MCI in 1998. A further EU/US positive comity agreement entered into force in June 1998.

From January 1994, with the entry into force of the European Economic Area Treaty, prohibitions corresponding to those of Article 85 and 86 of the Treaty of Rome, and the corresponding EU case law, came into effect in the member countries of the European Free Trade Area. Rules for cooperation on competition policy were also agreed as part of the *Europe Agreements* between the EU and the Associated Countries of Central and Eastern Europe, and the Commission have indicated that the enforcement of competition rules in those countries is to be regarded as one of the conditions of admission as full members of the Union.

The Commission has been pressing for the creation of a binding set of international competition rules, to be issued by the World Trade Organisation.

C   The direct impact on industrial structure and business behaviour

Competition policy has been only one of many influences upon industrial structure and business behaviour, and there have been few attempts

---

[17] See p. 169.

to isolate its contribution. Under these circumstances, the best that can be done is to examine past trends and consider what effects might plausibly be attributed to the direct impact of policy intervention.

Trends in the structure of United Kingdom industry

Industrial structure in Britain has been largely shaped by merger activity. In value terms the figures show a modest upward trend, on which is superimposed a series of very pronounced peaks of merger activity. As a percentage of total corporate assets, annual expenditures on acquisitions have varied from less than 1 per cent to over 8 per cent.

The first merger boom, which started at the end of the nineteenth century, brought together large numbers of firms into major horizontal combines in the textiles, chemicals, wallpaper, cement and soap industries. The second wave, in the 1920s, led to the creation of many of the firms which – on their own, or as components of subsequent mergers – came to dominate British manufacturing industry, including ICI, GEC, Metal Box, Fison, Unilever and Cadbury-Fry. Merger activity increased again in the 1950s, reaching a peak in the 1960s, bringing AEI and English Electric under the control of GEC, and bringing about unions of other large firms to create new giants such as Cadbury Schweppes, Rowntree Mackintosh, Allied Breweries, National Westminster and British Leyland. After subsiding to a comparatively low level in the early 1980s, spending on acquisitions began to rise again in 1984, and there was also a strong upward trend in divestments, transfers of subsidiaries and management buy-outs. Large, bitterly contested bids (such as the Guinness bid for Distillers) became more common, as did conglomerate divestments of product ranges to former rivals (such as Hanson's sale of Courage to Elders) or to the incumbent management.

The two prewar merger waves may have been motivated as much by the desire to achieve scale economies and to reap the advantages of nationwide marketing, as by the desire to gain market power. They nevertheless resulted in considerable accretions of market power in certain industries which, together with the formation of cartels and the erection of barriers against imports, afforded the firms concerned opportunities to protect themselves against competition. The postwar merger boom was probably encouraged for a time by the passing of the Restrictive Practices Act, as a result of which cartels and price rings were virtually prohibited, leaving mergers as an unregulated alternative means of limiting competition in the early 1960s. In the second half of the 1960s, however, the newly instituted mergers legislation began to have a slight restraining influence. Ten mergers were referred to the

Monopolies and Mergers Commission, of which four were found to be against the public interest, and two were abandoned (including Unilever/United Breweries, which was abandoned after being found not to be against the public interest). But a more important influence arose from the activities of the Industrial Reorganisation Corporation during that period in either providing financial support for mergers, or ensuring that they were not referred to the Commission. The direction of public policy during this period was uncertain, and its net effect was probably again to encourage mergers.

In the early 1970s there were signs that merger policy was beginning to bite. Some large horizontal mergers, such as Boots/Glaxo, were prohibited and it became evident that the Commission was becoming sceptical of claims that scale economies would necessarily contribute to efficiency. In the course of the 1970s, some 45 mergers were referred (some 2–3 per cent of those qualifying), of which 12 were found to be against the public interest and 16 were abandoned before inquiries were completed. It gradually became clear that – in the absence of mitigating factors such as entry prospects – there was a risk that any large merger creating combined market shares, much more than 40 per cent might be prohibited. That risk, together with the costs of failure (running, perhaps into tens of millions of pounds) must be presumed to have been a deterrent to many of those contemplating such mergers, as well as prompting the abandonment of some of those which were referred.

In the course of the 1970s and the first half of the 1980s, the British competition authorities also became involved in a number of contested mergers which did not raise significant competition issues (such as those involving Harrods and Sothebys). The threat of a merger reference came to be used by target managements as a means of defence, and the Commission frequently had to adjudicate between competing management claims. In retrospect, this can probably now be dismissed as a confused and inconclusive episode.

The 1980s saw a growth in the practice of incorporating divestiture and other undertakings into merger proposals in order to reduce their market-power implications and thereby to avoid a merger reference. The process of informal clearance by consultation with the Office of Fair Trading thereby assumed increasing importance, as compared with the formal procedures of the Monopolies and Mergers Commission. Similar undertakings have increasingly become a feature of informal negotiations with the European Commission, prior notification to whom has become normal practice for mergers with a possible Community dimension.

Market concentration (as measured, for example, by the total share of a market supplied by the five largest suppliers) rose markedly on average in the 1950s and 1960s, but levelled off and declined in the 1970s and 1980s.

Underlying influences

Important influences besides that of competition policy were at work, and many of the changes of industrial structure which have been reviewed may have originated from motives other than a desire to restrict competition. The integration of local soap manufacturers and the marketing of the product under national brand names, for example, seem to have occurred in response to scale economies available at the time, and to a demand for a product which could be relied upon not to cause skin damage. In a number of other British industries, developments in technology and marketing were a force for change: indeed the fact that increases in concentration tended to occur in the same industries in other industrialised economies suggests that they were the main driving force. Thus, it is possible that the creation of monopolies may at first have occurred in response to economic forces, and that the opportunities for exploitation which they provided may not have been realised until later.

Subsequent developments in technology and marketing may explain why the growth in concentration which occurred in the first half of the century and beyond did not persist into the 1970s and 1980s. Changes in technology have in the latter period often tended to reduce scale economies. Standardisation (as in the case of petrol) and the development of retailers' 'own brands' have reduced the importance of suppliers' brands. There has also been a growing awareness that the technical advantages of large-scale operation could he offset by disadvantages in other respects. Very large firms had been found to experience special difficulties in managing industrial relations and in responding to changing market conditions. E.F. Schumacher's dictum that 'small is beautiful' had found its way into corporate thinking.

Although nationwide monopolies remain, there has also been a progressive reduction in their market power. Competition from imports has made a very substantial impact. In the 1960s tariffs fell steeply on imports from all sources, and in the 1970s tariff barriers and quantitative restrictions upon imports from other members of the European Community were abolished altogether. There are now few manufacturing sectors in which imports do not make a significant contribution to competition. The market power of large British-owned firms has also been eroded by competition from foreign firms operating in the United Kingdom, which accounted by 1988 for some 20 per cent of British manufacturing output.

Intervention in the affairs of dominant firms

It is difficult to isolate the contribution which the competition authorities have made to the general lowering of barriers to competition. An indication can, however, be obtained by tracing the history of their intervention into the affairs of dominant firms.

British markets which, by the 1950s had come to be dominated by small groups of large firms included the national markets for glass, plasterboard, matches, electric cables, detergents, petrol and beer. The behaviour of dominant firms in most of those markets has been investigated from time to time by the competition authorities, and there has been official intervention on a number of occasions to prohibit acquisitions which those firms had proposed or to change some of their business practices. Those interventions, and their backgrounds, may be summarised as follows.

Glass

Pilkington Brothers was founded in 1826 as the St Helens Crown Glass Company. By 1905, it was the sole British manufacturer of plate glass and its only domestic competitor in the supply of sheet glass was Chance Brothers. In 1936 the two companies, which had for some years operated pricing agreements, set up a market-sharing agreement for cast glass, and by 1945, Chance had become a subsidiary of Pilkington. Domestic competition was thereby eliminated, and overseas competition was limited by a number of market-sharing and price-fixing agreements with continental manufacturers and with British glass merchants. In 1929, Pilkington and Triplex formed a joint company for the manufacture of safety glass, and Pilkington had acquired a controlling interest in Triplex by 1965 and full ownership by 1972 – eliminating thereby all domestic competition in that market. A Monopolies Commission report in 1968 approved the acquisition of Triplex and expressed confidence that Pilkington would not abuse its monopoly power,[18] but a subsequent report opposed Pilkington's proposed acquisition of the only UK supplier of mass-produced lenses.[19] Pilkington announced in 1957 that it had abandoned its price-fixing arrangements with British glass merchants, but

[18] *Flat Glass 1968.*
[19] *Pilkington/UKO 1977.*

admitted in 1988 that it had operated a price-fixing arrangement for double-glazing units between 1978 and 1984. In November 1990 the Restrictive Practices Court ruled that 12 price-fixing agreements covering stock float glass, toughened, laminated and silvered glass were against the public interest, and accepted undertakings from Pilkington and 40 other companies not to enforce such agreements.

Plasterboard

British Plasterboard was founded in 1917, and had by 1945 acquired most of the British capacity for the production of plasterboard and of its raw materials. In 1967 and 1968 it acquired all remaining British plasterboard manufacturing capacity from its two competitors. Neither acquisition was referred to the Monopolies Commission but a monopoly reference was made in 1972, in response to which the Commission offered no criticism of the way in which the company's monopoly position had been established, but expressed doubts about its efficiency and made recommendations as a result of which British Plasterboard eventually undertook in 1977 to abandon its system of uniform delivered prices.[20] On Britain's entry into the European Community in 1973, British Plasterboard announced the abandonment of restrictions upon imports from its associates in the Community, which they regarded as invalid under the Treaty of Rome. In 1988, however, the company was fined £2 million by the European Commission for operating a fidelity payments scheme and offering favourable delivery times to exclusive stockists.[21] In 1990 the Monopolies and Mergers Commission noted that, mainly as a result of the entry of Redland into the market, British Plasterboard's share of the market had fallen from 97 per cent to less than 75 per cent, and that there was vigorous price competition. On the Commission's recommendation, the 1977 undertakings concerning delivered prices were lifted.[22]

Matches

In 1861, Bryant and May, then UK agents of a Swedish company, started the manufacture under licence of safety matches. By the 1920s, all the other British match producers had been absorbed either into Bryant & May or into J. John Masters, which was by then under the control of Swedish Match. In 1927 Bryant & May and Masters combined to form

[20] *Plasterboard 1974.*
[21] Following the use by the Commission of their entry powers to get evidence of the obstruction of imports.
[22] *Plasterboard 1990.*

the British Match Corporation, a 33 per cent shareholding in which
went to Swedish Match. Agreements were set up for the sharing of
world markets, and the monopoly was further protected by restrictions
on the supply of match-making machinery.

A Monopolies Commission report[23] found those arrangements to be
against the public interest, and recommended the ending of restrictions
on the supply of match-making machinery, but not of most of the other
agreements. The report led to a renegotiation of those agreements but
the main links between Swedish Match and the British Match Corporation remained. In 1973 British Match acquired Wilkinson Sword, and
between 1978 and 1980 Alleghany International (an American domestic
appliance manufacturer) acquired the Wilkinson Match combine
including all of the Swedish Match holding – although Masters
remained under the day-to-day control of Swedish Match as their UK
agent. In 1987, Alleghany agreed to sell all of Wilkinson Match to
Swedish Match. The effect was to give the combined company total
control of 99 per cent of match manufacture, 82 per cent of match
distribution, and 42 per cent of the sales of disposable lighters, in the
UK. It was cleared by the Monopolies and Mergers Commission.[24] A
1992 report revealed profit rates on capital employed of over 200 per
cent and recommended price control in order to prevent Bryant & May
from earning excessive profits in the future.[25]

Electric cable

In 1945, the two largest British electric cable manufacturers merged to
form British Insulated Cables Ltd (BICC), accounting for around 25 per
cent of British production of insulated wires and cables, and with interests in copper-refining and electrical construction. BICC became the
leading member of the Cable Makers' Association which operated various
market-sharing and price-fixing schemes. In 1952, those schemes were
abandoned on the recommendation of the Monopolies Commission.[26]

Between 1955 and 1977 there were about a dozen further mergers and
BICC's share of UK production rose to 35 per cent. Among those mergers, BICC's acquisition of Pyrotenax, which gave it a 90 per cent share
of the UK market for mineral insulated cables was referred to the Monopolies and Mergers Commission and was cleared on the understanding
that the resulting cost savings would be used to expand sales and reduce

[23] *Matches 1953.*
[24] *Swedish Match/Alleghany 1987.*
[25] *Matches 1992.*
[26] *Insulated Wires and Cables 1952.*

prices, and that BICC would not operate a number of specified anti-competitive practices. (An undertaking then given to supply other manufacturers was unexpectedly taken up by GEC, giving it an advantage in other markets which has since been the subject of dispute.) The Commission found in 1979 that BICC's monopoly did not operate against the public interest, but that with three other suppliers, BICC had been operating an unregistered restrictive agreement concerning supplies of cable to the Post Office.[27] In an out-of-court settlement, the companies agreed to pay the Post Office £9 million in compensation.

Detergents

Lever Brothers (now Unilever) started soap manufacture in 1885 and pioneered the marketing of soap in Britain under national brand names. By 1920, having acquired several of its former competitors, Lever became UK market-leader. Under various market-sharing arrangements with Lever, ICI and Shell agreed not to enter the detergent market, but those arrangements had been abandoned by the early 1950s. Proctor and Gamble, a successful United States soap producer, made a substantial entry into the British market following its acquisition of Thomas Hedley in 1930. By the early 1960s, the two firms were supplying over 90 per cent of the British household detergents market.

In 1963 that situation was referred to the Monopolies Commission who reported that there was little price competition, that prices were unnecessarily high, and that entry was being deterred by excessive advertising expenditures. The Commission recommended that the companies should reduce their advertising expenditures by at least 40 per cent and their selling prices by around 20 per cent (*Household Detergents 1966*). Its recommendations were not accepted. The companies undertook instead to introduce new low-priced brands backed by relatively low-cost promotions. Those undertakings were amended and eventually abandoned in the 1970s in view of the increased buying power of the supermarket groups and of competition from their own brands. Advertising expenditures were, however, generally reduced in the 1970s and some price competition emerged, but the combined market share of the two companies declined by less than 8 per cent between 1964 and 1983.

Petrol

In 1964 the three leading suppliers, Shell/BP, Esso and Regent (now Texaco) supplied over 90 per cent of the UK petrol market and

---

[27] *Insulated Wires and Cables 1979.*

controlled 85 per cent of the retail sites by virtue either of ownership or of exclusive supply contracts. The Monopolies Commission inquiry at that time was, however, confined by its terms of reference to the question of the control of the retail outlets. As a result of their report,[28] the companies undertook to restrict the durations of exclusive supply agreements to five years, renewable annually thereafter. (Two restraint of trade cases at about the same time established that long-term agreements for the supply of petrol were unreasonable.) The companies also undertook to restrict the acquisition of further petrol stations, but were later released from that undertaking. Between 1964 and 1979, new suppliers had captured about a quarter of the market and the leading suppliers' shares of the market and of the number of controlled outlets dropped to below 66 per cent.

As the result of a further inquiry, the Commission found that the extent of the ownership of outlets was not then against the public interest, but suggested that the situation be kept under review by the Director-General of Fair Trading.[29] In 1983, the European Commission issued a block exemption for exclusive purchase agreements with petrol stations, lasting for up to ten years or for the duration of a tenancy if longer. In June 1988, a House of Commons Select Committee announced that it had found *prima facie* evidence of resale price maintenance at petrol stations, and on its recommendation, a further monopoly reference was made. The report of that inquiry noted that almost all retail outlets were still tied to suppliers, either by ownership or by exclusive supply agreements, but that there was no evidence of price collusion or of excessive profits.[30] The subsequent entry of supermarkets into petrol retailing has since contributed to a one-third fall in real pre-tax prices.[31]

Beer

The market for beer is characterised by extensive control of retail outlets by suppliers. (In the case of beer, however, the origins of that control lie in the operation in the nineteenth century of a restrictive licensing system intended to prevent 'social abuse'.) The merger boom of the 1960s brought together a number of regional brewers to form 'the big six'[32] who by 1969 supplied 68 per cent of the UK market, and owned

[28] *Petrol 1965.*
[29] *Petrol 1979.*
[30] *Petrol 1990.*
[31] *Petrol 1998.*
[32] (Bass, Allied, Whitbread, Watney, Courage and Scottish and Newcastle.)

about 50 per cent of all on-licences.[33] The brewers imposed 'ties' and exclusive purchasing arrangements upon those outlets, which the Monopolies Commission found in 1969 to be against the public interest.[34] The Commission's recommendation that the licensing laws should be relaxed was not implemented, but there are indications that they have since been administered less restrictively. No other remedies were proposed.

Between 1968 and 1972, there were some 15 further mergers involving the 'big six', none of which were referred to the Commission (although a projected merger between Unilever and Allied Breweries was abandoned after it had been referred and the Commission had cleared it). Three mergers involving Scottish and Newcastle have since been referred to the Commission, the first of which was abandoned, the second was cleared and the third[35] was stopped. The acquisitions of Courage, first by Imperial, then by Hanson, and then by Elders in 1986, were not referred. Between 1967 and 1986 the proportion of on-licences owned by brewers had fallen from 78 per cent to 56 per cent, but the domination of the 'big six' had increased to the point where they accounted for 75 per cent both of UK beer production and of brewer-owned premises.

Following a further reference in 1986, the Monopolies and Mergers Commission found there to be a complex monopoly situation which operated against the public interest by overcharging and restricting consumer choice.[36] The resulting Beer Orders required each brewer to untie half of all of its pubs in excess of 2000, either by sale or letting; to allow tied pubs to sell at least one of its competitors' beers, and to allow loan-ties to be terminated without penalty. In 1990 a merger between two of the 'big six', which was expected to lead to a market share of around 40 per cent was allowed, subject to undertakings designed to reduce the extent of local monopolies and exclusive purchasing ties. *(Elders/Grand Met 1990)*. In 1992 a further merger was allowed subject to similar undertakings *(Allied-Lyons/Carlsberg 1992)* and on further such undertakings the then Secretary of State allowed a merger between Scottish and Newcastle and Courage to go ahead without a reference to the Commission. That merger gave the merged company a market share of 28 per cent and left four national brewers with tied estates in

[33] Outlets – mainly public houses – licensed to sell beer for consumption on the premises.
[34] *Beer 1969.*
[35] With Elders IXL.
[36] *Beer 1989.*

the British market. In 1997 the Commission recommended – subject to further undertakings – approval of a merger which would have given the resulting firm a 37 per cent market share (*Bass/Carlsberg 1997*) but their recommendation was rejected by the then Secretary of State.

The consequences of intervention

The limited direct impact of the above interventions upon the markets in question can be ascribed in part to limitations upon the authorities' powers and resources. Many of the dominant firms concerned had achieved dominance before the present competition authorities existed, or before they had acquired their present powers of intervention. Effective action concerning existing monopolies must thereafter have been difficult to envisage. Any attempt to reduce the market power of the dominant firms by forced divestiture could have created industrial disruption on an incalculable scale, and systematic regulation of their commercial behaviour would in many cases have required a thoroughness of investigation and monitoring for which sufficient resources were not available. Action could be taken against overt cartels – and was taken, with great effect – but little could be done about the secret operation of cartels and other restrictive practices.

After 1965, however, powers were available to prevent dominant firms from augmenting their market power by mergers, but only limited use was made of them. The non-reference of many mergers, and the permissive attitude adopted towards many of those which were referred may have seemed justifiable on several grounds. In some cases, the dominant firm was already so powerful that the further acquisitions which were proposed would make little difference. In other cases, the authorities appear to have been influenced by the argument that large-scale operations were necessary in order to enable British firms to compete with overseas suppliers. In general, there was a disposition to accept estimates of efficiency gains and assurances of good behaviour, in the absence of convincing grounds for scepticism.

It would thus appear that, for a variety of reasons, the British competition authorities did not exert a decisive direct influence upon the major markets supplied by dominant firms. They may, nevertheless, have had an important indirect influence upon those and other markets. The mere risk of investigation may have deterred some of the largest companies from seeking to increase their market power by merger. Business practices which created artificial barriers to entry may also have been deterred by the risk of discovery and of investigations under which they might be condemned. It may have become clear to executives in large corporations that the competition authorities considered that the possession of market power carried with it a special obligation to refrain from anti-competitive and exploitative behaviour. The assurances of good behaviour that were given to the Commission may not always have been fully carried out, but they may have had a restraining influence on the corporate policy of those that gave them, and of others.

D Transparency, consistency and efficiency

Most of the work of the regulatory authorities is hidden from view, and most of their decisions are taken for reasons which are not published. This is necessarily true of the confidential advice which is given to individual companies by the Office of Fair Trading and the Competition Directorate of the European Commission. It is also true to a varying extent of their discretionary interpretation of published rules and guidelines. Only a small fraction of cases which met the statutory conditions for reference to the Monopolies and Mergers Commission were in fact referred, and the criteria for selection were not revealed. (Published guidelines then contained little beyond a summary of the legislation and a listing of the considerations which are taken into account.)

Lack of transparency in those respects may have limited the indirect impact of competition policy by engendering uncertainty concerning the circumstances under which the authorities are likely to intervene. Had that uncertainty been total, intervention by the authorities would have been universally regarded as an unpredictable business risk: but that was not the case. Managements of leading firms became aware that any overt action to enhance or exploit their market power would attract the attention of the authorities and that awareness must have exerted a substantial indirect influence on their business conduct. There was probably little indirect influence upon medium-sized firms. Thus, although there are very considerable areas of business conduct which have been decisively affected by the indirect influence of competition policy, there are also a number of important areas where its influence has been far from decisive. In those areas, intervention by the authorities has sometimes had the character of a business risk, which cannot be resolved except by an expensive case-by-case process of trial and error.

In recent years, however, the situation has improved. The Code of Practice on Access to Government Information which came into force in 1994 committed government departments and public bodies to volunteer information such as facts and analysis behind major policy decisions, as well as answering requests for information. This, together with the anticipated requirements of a forthcoming Freedom of Information Act, has had a considerable impact upon administrative practices, as regards – for example – the publication of internal documents, the production of explanatory guidelines and the issue of explanations for ministerial decisions.

In any assessment of the impact of policy upon the economy, the burden of cost and uncertainty which it has placed upon business has to be set against the benefits which it has conferred in promoting competition. The scale of the costs to business are likely to have been small[37] compared with the benefits to the economy, however. The welfare loss from monopolistic behaviour in the UK economy has been estimated to be at least 1 per cent of GDP (around £7.5 billion a year at 1996 prices).[38] A reduction by as little as a few per cent of that loss would probably have outweighed the costs of regulation. The legislative changes introduced in 1998, together with the recent improvements in transparency, will have further raised the excess of benefits over costs.

E   Conclusions

Although the evidence which has been reviewed in this chapter does not justify a confident assessment of the impact of competition policy, some tentative conclusions can be drawn. Among the least controversial must be the observation that the direct effects of the formal decisions of the regulatory authorities upon the firms which they have investigated amount in total to, at most, a minor influence upon the economy. The relatively small number of such decisions, fewer than 20 a year each by the European Commission and the Monopolies and Mergers Commission, would on its own justify such a conclusion. The vastly more numerous informal contacts which have taken place between firms and the regulatory authorities must also be assumed to have had a very limited total impact in view of the relatively insignificant numbers of staff involved. Thus if it is to be concluded that competition policy has had a significant influence upon the economy, that influence must have arisen from the effect of the decisions of the authorities upon the behaviour of businessmen at large.

Surprisingly, however, there is no hard evidence concerning the perceptions of businessmen as to the conduct which the regulatory

[37] See the DTI's Compliance Cost Assessment (Appendix 2).
[38] Fergusson & Fergusson 1988.

authorities are likely to find acceptable or unacceptable. The lack of published market research on that question might indeed be considered to be among the most remarkable aspects of the conduct of competition policy. In the absence of such evidence, assessment must depend upon an evaluation of the strength of the signals which the authorities have transmitted. On that question, however, the indications are mixed. On some practices such as retail price maintenance there has been a clear negative signal, masked only very slightly by 'noise'. On other practices, the signal is either very weak in itself or is heavily masked by the noise of apparently conflicting decisions.

Major contributions to improvements in the signal-to-noise ratio have come from the Community's block-exemption regulations. An exclusive dealing agreement which is drafted in accordance with the appropriate regulation, for example, is virtually certain of approval. The process by which those regulations are evolved has been very slow, however, and there are still gaps that remain to be filled.

Explanatory notices and guidelines have made further contributions. The regulations and guidelines which have been issued by the European Commission have for the most part followed the examples and precedents established by the published decisions of the regulatory authorities. Despite their comparatively minor direct impact, those decisions have thus been the ultimate source of the signals which have gone out to businessmen and of the noise which has accompanied them.

The ultimate impact of competition policy upon the economy must depend, however, upon the quality of the signals conveyed, as well as their strength. Quality has been determined by the skill and accuracy with which the authorities have balanced economic gains and losses in reaching their decisions. The few independent attempts which have been made to assess the quality of the authorities' decisions have for the most part been inconclusive or unconvincing, and it is doubtful whether an outsider can provide a reliable answer.

It seems beyond doubt, however, that influences other than competition policy have been more important, notably the increase in competition from abroad. The following assessment by the then Director-General of Fair Trading makes that point:

> Indeed, the power of international trade as a solvent of cartels and a disarmer of monopolies should not be underrated. Would that competition authorities were always as effective. Three very different examples will illustrate its power. The cement cartel survived two examinations by the Restrictive Practices Court but was finally

abandoned after several decades, in the face of imports from Greece and Spain, after those countries had joined the European Community. The plasterboard monopoly survived for many years after examination by the Monopolies and Mergers Commission, thanks to its tight hold on United Kingdom sources of gypsum, but it is now under challenge from a British company obtaining supplies of gypsum from elsewhere in the Community. And the Stock Exchange, having been forced to adapt to the globalisation of securities trading, bears little relationship to the body whose restrictive rule-book I challenged under the Restrictive Practices Act.[39]

Such developments lend support to the argument of the Austrian and Chicago Schools[40] that, given effective action to remove entry barriers, intervention by the competition authorities is largely unnecessary. There has indeed been pressure from industrial lobbies to limit the activities of the competition authorities on the grounds that overseas competition has already made their interventions unnecessary. The general consensus seems nevertheless to have favoured the strengthening, not the weakening, of competition policy.

[39] DGFT 1988.
[40] See pages 9 and 18.

9
The Future

A Internal developments

In terms simply of cost-effectiveness, the ideal outcome of the future development of competition policy would be a situation in which everyone knows what is likely to be prohibited, and no one is willing to risk infringement. In that ideal situation the authorities would have little to do beyond occasionally warning or reassuring a businessman who wishes to ascertain their reaction to a hitherto untested situation. Companies and taxpayers would thereby be relieved of the costs of unnecessary investigation and litigation.

Substantial progress toward that ideal may be expected as a result of the changes introduced in the UK in the closing years of the twentieth century. The abolition of the Restrictive Practices Act has put an end to a great deal of unnecessary bureaucratic activity in connection with commercial agreements, and the powers and penalties of the Competition Act have greatly reduced the attractiveness of evasion. The introduction of European Union precedents into domestic cases has reduced the uncertainties which were an inherent feature of the case-by-case approach of the various investigating groups of the former Monopolies and Mergers Commission. Insight into the regulators' attitudes is becoming easier as a result of the improvements in transparency which they have adopted and of the increased accessibility of information that is provided by the Internet. The progressive codification of precedents into regulations is continuing to clarify the authorities' concept of acceptable business conduct.

The European Commission's proposals to abolish the notification and exemption system are intended to relieve companies from unnecessary bureaucracy and allow the Commission to concentrate upon serious infringements. Moves toward the decentralised application of Community rules by national authorities and courts are also envisaged.

If cost-effectiveness were the only objective, prospects would appear good. The true objective of competition policy is not that simple, however. The broader ideal would be a regime that also promotes all of the efficiency advantages of competition without sacrificing any of the gains which are to be had from innovation and improved production methods. Apart from the fresh thinking surrounding the concept of contestability, the twentieth century saw little intellectual progress in the direction of that ideal. Assessments of the consequences of business practices still had to be built by subjective judgement upon the slender foundation of elementary economic theory and the work of the early antitrust authorities. Objective inquiries were rare.

Changes in the authorities' attitudes to vertical restraints are evidence, however, of a recently adopted willingness to question accepted beliefs, and there are other signs of a less introspective approach. It has recently become customary to seek, publish and analyse the views of businessmen and other policy outsiders about the desirability of change. It is to be hoped that this will be followed by assessment of the direct and indirect consequences of regulatory actions for businesses and for the economy in general.

Among the topics on which policy may develop is the treatment of luxury goods – using that term to denote products whose appeal arises from their high price. Sanction has already been given to refusal to supply to price-cutters for the purpose of preserving the luxury image of a wide range of products. Further difficult survey work on consumer preferences may be necessary to establish the boundaries of what can be regarded as luxury goods for that purpose. Suppliers of luxury products have not so far been seen as dominant, but that situation could change if the luxury end of a product range came to be seen as a market in its own right. While excessive pricing could not sensibly be regarded as an abuse of dominance in such a market, other abusive practices would fall within the scope of competition policy, and may raise fresh difficulties.

The rapid expansion of the Internet, and of Internet trading, will also pose intellectual and procedural challenges for the competition authorities. The network effect – by which the value of being connected increases non-linearly with the number of those already connected – is emerging as a powerful argument for a permissive attitude toward the acquisition of increased market share. (Of similar effect is the related tendency to 'lock-in', so that what was once the leading technology continues to be the dominant industry standard.) The authorities may consider it sensible to permit actions to promote dominance that would normally be prohibited in other contexts, but would then be under pressure to regulate more closely the exercise of such dominance. There have already been challenging examples of the use by cross-subsidisation of dominance in one such market, to acquire dominance in an associated market. The – already difficult – topic of predation may need further examination. The form of cross-subsidisation in which advertising receipts cover the cost of production is already commonplace in free newspapers and commercial television. It is now having a major influence upon Internet retailing, and it has even been proposed to use it to sell products at prices below those charged by the manufacturers.

There may also be a need for fresh thinking on the regulation of the public utilities. The last two decades of the twentieth century saw the introduction of competition into a number of activities hitherto considered to be the province of natural monopolies, and there may be room for further developments in that direction. Further opportunities to introduce competition may emerge as a result of the progressive liberalisation of public utilities within the Common Market. Where competition cannot do the job, there may be further progress toward a solution of the problem of regulating prices without discouraging innovation and productivity growth. Developments based on the precedents set by the European Commission – by which excessive prices have been detected by international comparisons within the Union – may sometimes prove more effective than regulation by profit limitation.

Productive new thinking in the UK may be furthered by the improvements that are being made to the career prospects of competition staff, and by the substitution of full-time professionals for the part-time services of 'the great and the good'.

B   External developments

It has been noted that the introduction of competition from abroad has been more effective than competition policy in maintaining and promoting economic efficiency. Further gains can be expected both from the development of the internal market within the European Union and from competition from outside. Regulatory action may, however, be needed to protect such gains. While the Internet will operate increasingly as a means of toppling trade barriers, it may also present regulatory problems on an international scale. The network-effect

favours international industrial concentration, and the Microsoft example has shown that a company whose practice is adopted as an international industry standard can thereby acquire immense market power.
There has so far been little need for international regulatory action,
except in respect of the supply of civil aircraft. The Boeing/McDonnell-
Douglas merger was recognised to raise regulatory issues on both sides of
the Atlantic, and its treatment demonstrated the advantages to be had
from collaborative arrangements such as had been set up between the
European Commission and the United States Department of Justice. In
the short- to medium-term there may be a proliferation and strengthening of such bilateral arrangements, but the development of a truly international antitrust system – operated, as the Commission has suggested,
by the World Trade Organisation – is very much a long-term prospect.

C   Independence and accountability

There may also be some changes in the balance between the legal and
the political characteristics of competition policy. The greater its impact
upon business, the stronger will be the case for treating it as part of the
legal system, concentrating its application upon competition issues, and
removing it from the lobbying pressures that are inherent in political
control. In the UK, the 1998 Competition Act was a move in that
direction, removing the wide-ranging 'public interest' criteria from
the operation of most aspects of competition policy, and removing
ministerial control from all but mergers decisions. The British government has announced its intention of taking the further step of reducing
the ministerial role in mergers policy but there have been hints of a
willingness to retain some non-competition criteria. To the extent that
European Commissioners are subject to national lobbying pressures,
there is also a case for replacing DGIV by a fully independent European
Cartel Office. The granting of independence to the Bank of England and
the European Central Bank suggests that opinion has moved in that
direction. Continued public acceptance may depend upon the adoption
of an effective form of accountability. Well-informed accountability is
difficult to achieve, however. The level of awareness of competition
policy is not high among business executives, and is negligible among
the population at large. Consequently, even the most carefully designed
survey is likely to produce erratic findings that appear biased in favour of
business. The contact group technique – under which a structured
sample of people are consulted after immersion in a comprehensive
course of objective information – may provide an answer.

Appendix 1   Terminology

Administrative letter   See *comfort letter* [41].

Advocate-General   A member of the Court of Justice of the same rank as a judge, who delivers an independent opinion before a judgement is made. [39]

Agent   A person or organisation that sells on behalf of a principal without owning the stocks that it sells or being responsible for unsold stocks. [114]

Allocative efficiency   The efficiency with which resources are allocated as between different products (as distinguished from *productive efficiency*). [8]

Ancillary restrictions doctrine   That restrictions that are necessary to the operation of a transaction that is not anti-competitive are not subject to the legislation that prohibits restrictive agreements. [112]

Areeda–Turner Rule   The rule that only if prices are set below *short-run marginal costs* should they be presumed to be predatory (see also *average variable cost*). [99]

Austrian School   A group of economists whose views include opposition to active regulatory intervention in the economy. [9]

Average variable cost   The average cost per unit of output, excluding those costs which remain constant in the short to medium term (used as a surrogate for short-run marginal cost in the *Areeda–Turner* criteria for predatory pricing). [99]

Avoidable costs   Costs which could be avoided by ceasing an operation suspected of being predatory, but excluding costs incurred in common with other operations, and sunk costs which were not incurred for the purposes of predation. [99]

Beta   The ratio of the variability of the price of a security to the variability of the total price of market as a whole (used in the *Capital Asset Pricing Model*). [105]

Blacklist   A list of practices which cannot be exempted, which appears in a *block exemption*. [22]

Block exemption   Closely defined conditions under which specified practices are exempt from Art. 81 of the Treaty of Amsterdam or from the Competition Act. [23]

Bundling   An arrangement under which products are sold only in stipulated combinations. A form of *tie-in sales*. (qv) [122]

Capital Asset Pricing Model (CAPM)   The theory that the rate of return which an equity investor expects from a particular security is given by the available riskless rate, plus the security's Beta, times the equity market's risk premium (that risk premium being the excess of the market's average return over the riskless rate). See Blake (1990), p. 297. [105]

Captive customers   Those who are unable to switch purchases in favour of a substitute. [64]

Certainty Equivalent Accounting Rate of Return (CARR)   A rate of return measure (devised by Graham and Steele) which may be compared with the risk-free cost of capital in order to identify excessive pricing. [105]

Chain of substitution   Extension of a market by progressive switching. [64]

Clearance   See *negative clearance*.

College of Commissioners   The collective decision-making body of the European Commission. [37]

Comfort letter   An official statement that no further action is envisaged. [41]

Comity of Nations   The mutual recognition by countries of the laws and customs of others. [55]

Common costs   Costs which would not be reduced if a firm ceased supplying one of a group of products.

Community dimension   The condition, stated in Regulation 4064/89, for a merger to come under EU jurisdiction. [27]

Complex monopoly   A condition defining jurisdiction over collaborating groups in the Fair Trading Act 1973. [32]

Concentration   EU terminology that is synonymous with merger. [26]

Concentration ratio   A ratio which indicates the degree to which an industry is dominated by its larger firms. The five-firm concentration ratio, for example, is the ratio of the combined output of the top five firms to the output of the industry as a whole. A more comprehensive measure is provided by the *Herfindahl Index* (sometimes termed the *Herfindahl–Hirschman Index* or *HHI*, which is the sum of the squares of the market shares of all of the firms in the industry (H $= \sum_n f_n^2$ where f_n is firm n's share of industry output, and H ranges from 0 to 1 where f is a ratio, or 10000 to 1 where f is a percentage).

Confidential guidance   OFT advice as to whether a merger is likely to be referred. [49]

Conformance programme   A system by which a company trains and informs members of its staff about the relevant requirements of the competition regulations (the existence of which may affect penalties for infringements). [Preface]

Contestability   An approach to the market condition of perfect contestability, in which entry and exit are costless. [10]

Copyright   An exclusive property right in an original book, film, composition, etc. which belongs automatically to its author or anyone to whom he assigns it (see also *patent, design right*). [129]

Cost of capital   The weighted average cost of equity and debt to a company. [105]

Cross-price elasticity   The effect on sales of Y of a change in the price of X. [64]

Design right   An exclusive property right over an original design and over articles made to that design which belongs automatically to the designer if he works on his own or otherwise to the person who employed him or commissioned him to produce that design. [129]

DGIV   Abbreviation for Directorate General IV, the competition department of the European Commission. [37]

Dominance   Economic strength enabling its possessor to act independently of competitors and customers. [69]

Economies of scale   Factors which cause the average cost of making a product to fall as the rate of output of the product rises. [111]

Economies of scope   Factors that make it cheaper to produce a range of related products than to produce each on its own. [111]

Essential facility   A facility to which access is essential in order to compete in a market, the duplication of which is extremely difficult. [130]

Exclusive dealing   Includes *exclusive purchasing* (in which a supplier does not allow his distributors to deal in his competitors' products) and *exclusive selling* (in which a distributor does not allow his suppliers to supply other distributors). [120]

Exemption   An official decision that an agreement is not prohibited under Article 81(1) because it meets the requirements of Article 81(3). [22]

Externalities   Consequences for welfare which are not reflected in costs and prices. [5]

False positive diagnosis   Diagnosis of a detriment where none exists. [97]

Foreclosure   Conduct by a dominant firm which excludes others from a market.

Franchise   An agreement under which a legally independent *franchisee* makes or sells a product under the brand name of a *franchisor* and to his specification, usually with his marketing and other support. [113]

Free rider   A firm that takes advantage of another's investment, e.g. in promoting the sales of a product. [111]

Full-function joint venture   One that has all the resources necessary for its function, including funding, staff and tangible and intangible assets. [27, 87]

Full-line forcing   A condition of supply that the purchaser buys the full range of a particular class of the supplier's products. [122]

Gray market   See *parallel imports*.

Herfindal Index   See *concentration ratio*.

Horizontal transactions   Transactions between competitors. [9]

Issues letter   See *public interest letter*.

Joint venture   A business arrangement in which two companies invest in a project over which both have partial control (see also *full-function*). [86]

Know-how   Secret technical information not protected by patents or design rights.

Leverage of market power   The use of market power in one market to create market power in another.

Lock-in   A situation in which purchasers cannot switch to a preferable product because of the costs of making a change (including costs arising from *network effects* and *path dependency*). The continued use of the QWERTY keyboard is the conventional example. [70]

Long-run marginal cost   The cost of increasing output by one unit over a sustained period including the cost of increasing output capacity. [99]

Marginal cost   The cost of producing one additional unit of output. [91]

Market for corporate control   The theory that mergers provide a market in which managers compete. [77]

Market power   The ability to influence prices. [6]

Market share   The fraction of the total sales of a product supplied by a firm. Normally measured in terms of sales value.

Merger situation   The conditions which determine merger jurisdiction under the Fair Trading Act 1973. [27]

Monopoly situation   A definition which limits jurisdiction over a single company under the Fair Trading Act. [31]

Nash equilibrium   A theoretical situation in which each competitor in a market pursues his best strategy in the knowledge of the strategies of all the other competitors.

Natural monopoly   An industry in which the relation between the technology and the market is such that productive efficiency is greatest when there is only one producer.

Negative clearance An official declaration that an agreement falls outside the scope of Art. 81(1) or that a practice falls outside the scope of Art. 82. [40]

Network effect The fact that the value of a network to its users increases non-linearly with the numbers connected to it. [70]

Notification An application in respect of a commercial agreement for immunity from action by the authorities. [39]

Official Journal See the European Commission in Appendix 2.

Oligopolistic market A market dominated by a few suppliers. [6]

Opposition procedure A procedure which applies to specified types of agreements, under which a notified agreement is deemed to be exempt unless the authorities raise an objection within a specified time. [41]

Optimal resource allocation A situation in which there can be no reallocation of resources which would make anyone better off without making someone worse off. [5]

Parallel exemption Applies to agreements that are exempt from Chapter 1 of the Competition Act 1998 by virtue of having been exempted under Art. 81(3) of the Treaty of Amsterdam. [24]

Parallel imports A flow of imports from a low-price source into a high-price country which is additional to the normal flow of imports generated by the manufacturers and traders. A form of arbitrage which tends to remove price differences. [111]

Patent The grant of an exclusive right (subject to statutory limitations) to the use and benefit of a new and non-obvious idea that is capable of industrial exploitation (see also *copyright, design rights*).

Path dependence The influence upon an existing market position of economic forces that no longer exist – such as the effect of a disused port upon an adjacent road network. Path dependence sometimes accounts for the continued dominance of a product – such as the QWERTY keyboard – despite competition from superior products (see *lock-in*).

Perfect competition A situation in which all market shares are small, there is no collusion and no entry barrier, and the products are homogeneous. [4]

Predation/predatory behaviour The acceptance of losses which are incurred in order to eliminate a competitor so that increased profits can be earned in the future, or in order to deter future entry. [98]

Predatory pricing Setting prices at below cost in order to eliminate competitors (see *Areeda–Turner*). [98]

Privileged information Information such as is exchanged between a lawyer and his client.

Productive efficiency The efficiency with which resources are combined to produce a specific product (as distinguished from *allocative efficiency*). [5]

Public interest The criterion stated in the Fair Trading Act. [30]

Public interest letter A list, sent to the parties concerned, of the issues which the Competition Commission wishes to examine. [53]

Qualifying merger A merger that is within the scope of EU Regulation 4064/89. [27]

Quantity forcing A requirement that a retailer must buy at least a stipulated minimum quantity of goods.

Rapporteur A DGIV case-handler.

Real rate of return The rate of return corrected for inflation.

Regulator   The Director-General of: Telecommunications, Gas or Electricity Supply, or Water Services; or the Rail Regulator.

Resale price maintenance   A requirement that distributors do not sell at below a stipulated price. [113]

Return on capital employed (ROCE)   Operating profit as a percentage of total of shareholder's capital and retained profit, revaluation reserves, borrowings less cash balances and minority interests.

Second-best, theory of   A theory which establishes that, if one of the conditions for optimal efficiency is unattainable, a situation in which all of the other conditions are met is not necessarily the best alternative. [7]

Se*lective distribution*   The practice on the part of a supplier of limiting the outlets through which his product may be sold by the imposition of qualitative or quantitative criteria. [117]

Short-run marginal cost   The cost of increasing output by one unit when this does not require an increase in output capacity. [99]

Spillover   Effects on competition resulting from the coordination of the activities of the parents of a joint venture, other than through the joint venture. [87]

Stand-alone cost   The least cost that would be incurred by a hypothetical efficient competitor, supplying the product on its own from a fully-utilised plant of optimum size. [104]

Structural joint venture   A joint venture involving a substantial amount of new investment. [88]

Sunk costs   Costs which cannot be recovered when a firm leaves a market. [11]

Supply-side substitution   Entry into a product market of a competitor who switches existing capacity to the supply of the product. [66]

Tie-in sales   A condition of supply for a product that the purchaser must also buy another product. [122]

Trademark   A symbol identifying the article on which it appears with a particular supplier.

Undertaking   (1) EU parlance for a company or any other organisation producing goods or services; (2) a promise concerning future conduct.

Vertical transactions   Transactions between manufacturers and retailers or licensees and licensors. [9]

Warning letter   A statement of regulatory concern. [41]

Welfare, economic (or social)   The total well-being of a community. (Welfare cannot be measured, but increases and decreases can be identified.) [6]

Appendix 2   Legislation, Guides and Other Official Publications

A   Legislation

The full texts of recent legislation are available on the internet:

The Competition Act 1998: http://www.oft.gov.uk
Statutory Instruments implementing the Competition Act http://www.dti.gov.uk
The Treaty of Amsterdam and Community Regulations: http://europa.eu.int.
Articles in the Rome Treaty were replaced by different numbering in the
Amsterdam Treaty as follows:

Rome	28	30	34	36	37	81	85	86	90
Amsterdam	26	28	29	30	31	77	81	82	77

Copies of the Fair Trading Act 1973 and other legislation can be obtained from
the Stationery Office, Publications Centre, PO Box 276 London SW8 5DT,
tel.: 0171 873 9090, fax: 0171 873 8200

B   Guides and other publications

1.   The European Commission

Address: Commission of the European Communities, 150 Avenue de Cortenberg,
1050 Brussels, Belgium.
DGIV's URL: http://europa.eu.int/comm/dg04/public/en/index.htm

All of the following publications are available on DGIV's website or from The
Stationery Office International Sales Agency, tel.: 0171 873 90 90, fax: 0171 873
84 63

The Official Journal, L series (legislation, daily)
Regulations, decisions and directives reproduced in full on all topics; a competi-
tion decision typically covers 10 to 80 pages.
The Official Journal, C series (communications, daily)
Information, Commission notices, bald statements of Court judgements and
Commission decisions.
The Bulletin of the European Communities (monthly, about 100 pages)
Short (10- to 30-line) summaries of Commission decisions, etc., on competition
and all other topics.
Report on Competition Policy (annual, 330 to 500 pages)

Summaries of all Commission and Court decisions, detailed analyses of the treatment of selected aspects of mergers and business practices, summaries of competition policy activities in member states.

Competition Policy Newsletter (quarterly, about 80 pages)

More detailed summaries and commentaries. A particularly valuable feature is provided by regular articles by members of DGIV under the heading of 'Recent Developments and Important Decisions'.

Also obtainable, subject to commercial confidentiality: copies of undertakings and selected comfort letters.

2.   The European Court of Justice

Address: Palais de Cour de Justice, Boulevard Konrad Adenaur, Kirchberg, L-2925 Luxembourg, tel. (352) 4303.1 URL: http://www.curia.eu.int

Decisions of the Court.

3.   The Office of Fair Trading

Address: Field House, 15–25 Breams Buildings, London EC4A 1P R, tel: 0171 211 8000, fax: 0171 211 8800

E-mail: enquiries@oft.gov.uk URL: http://www.oft.gov.uk.

Publications from: PO Box 366, Hayes, UB3 1XB, tel: 0870 60 60 321, fax: 0870 60 70 321

or: Stationery Office Ltd, Publications Centre, PO Box 276, London SW8 5DT, tel.: 0171 873 0011, fax: 0171 873 8200.

Report of the Director-General (annual, 70 to 90 pages)

A personal statement followed by factual summaries of UK competition policy cases and important EU cases (together with material relating to consumer protection).

Guides:

The Competition Act 1998, a series of guides:

> *The Major Provisions; The Chapter 1 Prohibition, The Chapter II Prohibition*
> *Market Definition, De Minimis, Dual Notifications, EC Comfort Letters*
> *Investigation and Enforcement Procedures*
> *Concurrent Application to the Regulated Industries*
> *Rights of Appeal*
> *Assessment of Individual Agreements and Conduct*
> *Assessment of Market Power*
> *Mergers and Ancillary Restraints*
> *Application to the Telecommunications Sector*

Mergers: a guide to procedures under the Fair Trading Act 1973

Merger Submissions: a briefing note

4.   The Competition Commission

Address: New Court, 48 Carey Street, London WC2A 2JT, tel.: 0171 324 1467, fax: 0171 324 1400

E-mail: mmc@gtnet.gov.uk , URL: http://www.open.gov.uk/mmc

Summaries of recent reports of the former Monopolies and Mergers Commission are available on the Commission's website and copies of all reports are available at The Westminster Reference Library, 35 St Martin's Lane, London WC2H 7HP.

5. The Department of Trade and Industry

Address: The Competition Policy Division, Department of Trade and Industry, 1–19 Victoria Street , London SW1 0ET, tel.: 0171 215 6035/6772, fax: 0171 215 6565   URL: http://www.dti. gov.uk.
Draft statutory instruments implementing the Competition Act
Compliance cost assessment and regulatory appraisal of the Competition Bill 1998
Guide: DTI procedures for handling merger references
Press releases announcing merger references, clearances and other decisions by the Secretary of State.

6. The OECD

Address: Competition Law & Policy Division , OECD, 2 Rue André Pascal 75775 Paris
E mail: dafccp.contact@oecd.org, URL: http://www.oecd.org/daf/ccp
Research reports, reviews of competition policy in member states, etc.

7. The US Department of Justice, Antitrust Division

Address: 950 Pennsylvania Avenue NW, Washington DC 20530–0001
Email: web@usdoj.gov. URL: http://www.usdoj.gov/atr/index.html
Cases, guidelines, announcements, etc.

List of Cases

References

Areeda and Turner (1975) 'Predatory Pricing and Related Practices under Section 2 of the Sherman Act: a Comment', *Harvard Law Review*, 697, 1975.

Areeda and Turner (1978) *Antitrust Law*, Little, Brown & Co.

Baumol, W.J (1961) 'Economic Theory and Operations Analysis', Prentice Hall, pp. 207–17.

Baumol, W.J (1982) 'Contestable Markets', *The American Economic Review*, Vol. 72, No. 1, March 1982.

Baumol, W.J., L.C. Panzar, and R.D. Willig (1982) *Contestable Markets and the Theory of Industry Structure*, Harcourt Brace Jovanovich.

Bellamy, C.W. and G.D. Child (1987) *Common Market Law of Competition*, Sweet & Maxwell.

Blake, D. (1990) *Financial Market Analysis*, McGraw-Hill.

Bloom, M. *The OFT's Role in the New Regime*. Speech at the Centre for the Law of the European Union, 10 September 1998 (http://www.oft.gov.uk./html/rsearch/sp-arch/regime.htm)

Bork, R.H. (1978) *The Antitrust Paradox: a Policy at War with Itself*, Basic Books Inc.

Borrie, Sir G. (1991) Evidence to the House of Commons Trade and Industry Committee Session 1991–2, lst report: Takeovers & Mergers.

Carlsberg, B. (1988) *The Control of British Telecommunications Prices*, Office of Telecommunications.

Chiplin, B. and M. Wright (1987) *The Logic of Mergers*, Hobart Paper No. 107, Institute of Economic Afrairs.

Cini, M. and L. McGowan (1998) *Competition Policy in the European Union*, Macmillan.

Comp Rep (No.) (Year) *The Annual Report on Competition Policy*, Commission of the European Union.

DGFT (Year) *The Annual Report of the Director-General of Fair Trading*, HMSO.

Dobson, P.W., and M. Waterson (1996) *Vertical Restraints and Competition Policy*, OFT Research Paper No. 12

Dobson, P.W., M. Waterson, and A. Chu (1998) *The Economic Analysis of Buying Power*, OFT Research Paper 16.

Elliott, D.C. and L.D. Gribbin (1977) 'The Abolition of Cartels and Structural Change in the United Kingdom' in Jaquemine and de Jong (eds) *Welfare Aspects of Industrial Markets*, Leiden.

Fairburn, L.A. and L.A. Kay (eds) (1989) *Mergers and Mergers Policy*, Oxford University Press.

Fergusson, P. and G. Fergusson (1988) *Industrial Economics: Issues and Perspectives*, cited in the DTI Compliance Cost Assessment (see Appendix 2).

Friedman, M. (1966) *Essays in Positive Economics*, Phoenix Books.

George, K. (1989) 'Do We need a Mergers Policy?' in Fairburn and Kay, op. cit.

Goyder, D.G. (1992) *EC Competition Law*, Clarendon Press.

Graham, M. and A. Steele *The Assessment of Profitability by the Competition Authorities*, FT Research Paper No. 10. February 1997.

Green, N. (1986) *Commercial Agreements and Competition Law*, Graham & Trotman.

Haag, M. and R. Klotz (1998) 'Commission Practice Concerning Excessive Pricing in Telecommunications in Competition Policy', *Newsletter*, June 1998.

Holl, P. and L.F. Pickering (1986) *The Determinants and Effects of Actual, Abandoned and Contested Mergers*, UMIST mimeo (referred to in DTI 1988).

Howe, M. (1988) 'Franchising and Restrictive Practices Law' *European Competition Law Review*, Vol. 9, Issue 4.

Howe, M. (1994) *Recent Developments in United Kingdom Competition Law and Policy*, and Proceedings of the 13th Annual Anti-Trust Law Conference, Robinson College, Cambridge, 27–30 September 1994.

House of Commons (1995) *UK Policy on Monopolies*, Session 1994–95, Trade and Industry Committee. Fifth Report. 1IC 249.HMSO, London.

HM Treasury (1991) *Economic Appraisal in Central Government*, HMSO.

Kiriazis, G. (1998) 'Positive Comity in EU/US Cooperation', *Competition Policy Newsletter* No. 3, October 1998.

Korah, V. (1997) 1997 *EC Competition Law and Practice* 6th edition, Hart Publishing.

Little, I.D.M. (1957) *A Critique of Welfare Economics*, Oxford University Press.

Littlechild, S.C. (1986) *The Fallacy of the Mixed Economy*, Hobart Paper No. 80, Institute of Economic Affairs.

Livy *The Early History of Rome*, tr. de Selincourt, Penguin Classics, 1960.

Meade, LS. (1968) 'Is the New Industrial State Inevitable?' *Economic Journal* 78, p. 372.

Morrison, S.A. and C. Winston (1987) 'Empirical Implications and Tests of the Contestability Hypothesis', *Journal of Law and Economics*, Vol. XXX, April 1987.

NERA 1992 'Market Definition in UK Competition Policy, OFT Research Paper No. 1, 1992.

Neven, D., R. Nuttall and P. Seabright (1993) *Merger in Daylight*, Centre for Economic Policy Research, London.

OECD (1989) *Competition Policy and Intellectual Property Rights*. Organisation for Economic Cooperation and Development, Paris.

Ravenscroft, D. and F.M. Scherer (1988) *Mergers, Sell-offs and Economic Efficiency*, Brookings Institute.

Reekie, W.D. (1979) *Industry, Prices and Markets*, Phillip Alan.

Schaub, A. (1998) 'International Cooperation in Antitrust Matters', *Competition Policy Newsletter*, February 1998.

Scherer, F.M. (1990) *Industrial Structure and Market Performance*, Rand McNally.

Schwartz, M. (1986) 'The Nature and Scope of Contestability Theory', Oxford Economic Papers 38, pp. 37–57.

Swann, D. *et al.* (1974) 'Competition in British Industry. Restrictive Practices Legislation' in *Theory and Practice*, Unwin University Books.

Van Gerven, G. and E.N. Varin (1994) 'The Woodpulp Case and the Future of Concertation Practice', *Common Market Law Review*, Vol. 31, No. 3, June 1994.

Whish, R. (1993) *Competition Law*, 3rd edition, Butterworth.

Williamson, O. (1987) *Antitrust Economics*, Blackwell.

Winch, D.M. (1971) *Analytical Welfare Economics*, Penguin.

Index